Telecourse Study Guide
for
A
Writer's

Telecourse Study Guide
for
A
Writer's

HARRYETTE BROWN
Content Specialist

Produced by:

 Dallas Telecourses

Dallas County Community College District

in cooperation with

HarperCollins*CollegePublishers*

and

PBS Adult Learning Service

The telecourse, *A Writer's Exchange*, is produced by the Dallas County Community College District, R. Jan LeCroy Center for Educational Telecommunications, in cooperation with HarperCollins College Publishers and the PBS Adult Learning Service.

Special thanks are extended to every one at the R. Jan LeCroy Center for Educational Telecommunications who participated in the production of *A Writer's Exchange*, especially to Nora Coto Busby, Instructional Designer, and Betsy Turner, Print Specialist. For their assistance in the production of *A Writer's Exchange*, we express our appreciation to Pamela K. Quinn, Vice President, R. Jan LeCroy Center for Educational Telecommunications; Paul Bosner, Project Director; Hector DeLuna, Producer; Phillip Johnson, Producer/Director; Laura Bohlcke, Production Assistant; Kimberly Allison, Research Assistant; and to the Local and National Advisory Committees: Dr. Joanne Bryant, Dr. Sam Dragga, Dr. Tahita Fulkerson, Dr. Gwendolyn Gong, Professor Carol Johnson, Dr. Phillip Sipiora, Professor Richard F. Tracz, Professor Martina Agbanyo, Dr. Rea Bell, Dr. Susan Faulkner, Professor Dorothy Good, Professor Dee Dee Hinojosa, Dr. Paul Hunter, and Dr. Mike Sink.

—Harryette Brown

This edition has been printed directly from camera-ready copy.

ISBN 0-06-502520-2

Contents

* Indicates lessons without accompanying video.

Introduction

"The only section left for you is the telecourse. Do you think you can teach writing to students who are not in a classroom and who will get much of their instruction from a television set?"

Of course not, I thought, as I listened to these words of my department chair replying to my belated request to teach an extra section of composition. I had been told that my college would be offering a writing telecourse in the fall of 1974, but I had dismissed the idea of teaching such a course. I felt that students needed to be in a classroom with other students—and with me—to learn to write well. I considered teaching the course only because I needed some extra money to pay my son's unexpected medical bills. Reluctantly, I agreed to try the telecourse section just that one semester.

Twenty-plus years later, the toddler who needed tubes in his ears is a college graduate, but I am still teaching students to write without benefit of a traditional classroom. My initial skepticism about the validity of teaching and learning at a distance was overcome the first semester I tried it as I saw the progress my students made through the course. In subsequent years, I have become convinced that the important components of learning are the student, the teacher, and the instructional materials rather than the classroom space itself. My students have taught me that they can learn when given the opportunity, the attention of a caring teacher, and materials that are instructive and interesting. That is why I became involved in the production of *A Writer's Exchange*. I know that students learn from a combination of video programs, a study guide, a textbook, and an involved, on-site teacher. I believe that current video and computer technology will make learning to write outside the traditional classroom even more desirable for many students who find such classrooms unavailable to them.

The design team of *A Writer's Exchange* has attempted to design a course that will give you everything you would get in a traditional classroom, and more. In addition to interaction with your classmates and teacher (by mail or by e-mail), you will be able to go to the places where writing really takes place, to the classrooms and workplaces where people use writing every day. You will hear experienced writers explain how they solve the problems that each writing task involves.

You will hear more than a dozen expert researchers and teachers of writing from all parts of the United States share their experience and knowledge about writing. You will learn about the history and theory of rhetoric, the academic discipline that has been the cornerstone of higher education since the Middle Ages.

I have tried to incorporate what I have learned over the years as a teacher of writing to distance learners into *A Writer's Exchange*. In contrast to my feelings about distance education in 1974, I am now certain that students can learn to write in their homes and workplaces as well as in a traditional classroom.

I hope *A Writer's Exchange* encourages, interests, and challenges you.

—Harryette Brown

Course Organization

A *Writer's Exchange* is designed as a comprehensive learning package consisting of three elements: a study guide, a textbook, and video programs. In addition to these essential elements, a handbook and computer software are available to support and enhance the learning system.

STUDY GUIDE

The study guide for this course is:

Harryette Brown. *Telecourse Study Guide for A Writer's Exchange.* New York: HarperCollins College Publishers, 1995.

The study guide acts as your daily instructor. Each lesson begins with the Lesson Assignment to allow you to schedule your time appropriately. Following the assignment is the Overview, which provides you with a brief introduction and a context for the material presented in that lesson. The Overview ends with specific Lesson Objectives and Goals for the lesson. The Text Assignment lists points designed to help you get the most from your reading. In the twenty-two (22) lessons that include a video, the Video Assignment outlines points that will help you learn from the video presentation. (For your information, the video program expert for each lesson is identified in the appendix.) The four lessons that do not include a video suggest activities that will be helpful to you at the point in the course at which the lesson occurs.

If you follow the study guide recommendations for each lesson carefully, you should successfully accomplish all of the requirements for this course.

TEXTBOOK

In addition to the study guide, a rhetoric textbook is required for this course:

Gwendolyn Gong and Sam Dragga. *A Writer's Repertoire*. New York: HarperCollins College Publishers, 1995.

The text explains rhetorical principles and suggests specific writing strategies. It includes many examples of student essays as well as professional essays from a variety of fields. Reference chapters highlight research techniques, test-taking strategies, and commonly used style and usage information. The text includes directions for writing assignments that grow from the rhetorical theories in the text.

HANDBOOK

A supplemental handbook is also recommended to provide information and exercises about specific issues in writing, grammar, and usage:

Maxine Hairston and John Ruszkiewicz. *The Scott, Foresman Handbook for Writers*. Current edition. New York: HarperCollins College Publishers.

The handbook includes a complete reference handbook on matters of usage, grammar, punctuation, and style. It also includes information on the writing process and research strategies along with information on major documentation formats.

VIDEO PROGRAMS

The course includes twenty-two video programs in the twenty-six lessons. Each video program is correlated with the study guide and the reading assignment for that lesson. Be sure to read the Video Assignment section in the study guide before you watch the program. The video programs include three or four brief case studies reflecting the skills being taught in the lesson. Each program showcases a well-known professor who comments on the case studies and explains how the information in each segment can be used by writing students.

   If the programs are broadcast more than once in your area, or if video or audio tapes are available at your college, you might find it helpful to watch the video programs more than once or to listen to an audio tape for review. You may wish to record each program for further study and review.

Study Guidelines

Follow these guidelines as you study the material presented in each lesson:

1. LESSON ASSIGNMENT—
   Review the Lesson Assignment in order to schedule your time appropriately. Pay careful attention; the titles and numbers of the textbook chapter, the study guide lesson, and the video program may be different.

   • Special Note:
   You will be directed to "read" some text and handbook assignments and "review" others.
   Assignments with the "read" direction provide new information for the lesson and should be read by all students.
   Assignments with the "review" direction may or may not be required by your instructor, but they provide reference information for the lesson and should be read by those students who want further clarifications or illustrations.

2. OVERVIEW—
   Read the Overview for an introduction to the lesson material.

3. LEARNING OBJECTIVES—
   Review the Learning Objectives and pay particular attention to the lesson material that relates to them.

4. TEXT ASSIGNMENT—
   To get the most from your reading, review the Text Assignment section of the study guide, then read the assignment. You may want to write responses or notes to reinforce what you have learned.

5. VIDEO ASSIGNMENT—
   To get the most from the video segment of the lesson, review the Video Assignment section of the study guide, then watch the video. You may want to write responses or notes to reinforce what you have learned.

6. RELATED ACTIVITIES—
Related Activities are not required unless your instructor assigns them. They are offered as suggestions to help you learn more about the material presented in the lesson.

7. WRITTEN ASSIGNMENT—
- Obtain your written assignment from your instructor.
- Review your writing assignment for the lesson.
- Work on your writing assignment, using the text, handbook, video, your peers, and your instructor as resources. Remember to ask for help when you need it.
- Send your writing assignment to your classmates or your instructor as your syllabus tells you.

Lesson 1

Rhetorical Heritage, Modern Applications

LESSON ASSIGNMENT

Review the following assignment in order to schedule your time appropriately. Pay careful attention; the titles and numbers of the textbook chapter, the study guide lesson, and the video program may be different from one another.

Text:
>Gong and Dragga, *A Writer's Repertoire,*
>Read Chapter 1, "Rhetoric and Writing: Background and
>   Concepts," pp. 3–36.

Handbook:
>Hairston and Ruszkiewicz, *The Scott, Foresman Handbook for Writers,*
>Refer to all sections in the following chapter:
>   Chapter 1

Video:
>View "Rhetorical Heritage, Modern Applications"
>from the series, *A Writer's Exchange.*

OVERVIEW

"Rhetorical Heritage, Modern Applications" introduces you to the study of the subject that has formed the basis of higher education in Western civilization since ancient times. You will learn that the term *rhetoric* means much more than empty or deceptive language: the term also refers to the skillful use of language; to a subject for study and research; and to a practical, applied art. In this lesson, you will see how rhetoric developed from the days of Aristotle to the present. You will find out how ancient concepts such as the five canons of rhetoric can help you improve your writing today. You will also meet a contemporary rhetorician whose theories help us define why we are writing and thus clarify how to proceed with our writing tasks.

When you have finished the lesson, you will know what the term *rhetoric* means as an academic discipline and an applied art. You will also know the general outline of the development of rhetoric from its roots in ancient Greece. You will understand key terms that are often used in discussions of rhetoric, and you will understand how clarifying our aim in writing helps us to approach any writing task.

LEARNING OBJECTIVES

Goal

You should be able to approach rhetoric both as an academic discipline and an applied art, and understand key terms and concepts that will be used in subsequent lessons: rhetoric, the canons of rhetoric, the rhetorical situation (writer, reader, subject), historical framework, and the "territory of rhetoric," both oral and written.

Objectives

Upon completing this lesson, you should be able to:

1. Define the term *rhetoric* from its historical and contemporary perspective.

2. Differentiate the positive connotations of the term *rhetoric* from the popular negative connotations.

3. Explain the relationship between the oral and written components of the "territory of rhetoric."

4. Place the five canons of rhetoric in the historical context of classical Western civilization.

5. Explain the three types of appeals to the audience: *ethos*, *pathos*, and *logos*.

6. Redefine the five canons of rhetoric (invention, arrangement, style, memory, delivery) in both classical and contemporary terms.

7. Explain the key parts of the rhetorical situation (writer, reader, subject).

8. Relate the aims of writing to the communication triangle.

9. Differentiate between knowledge by participation and knowledge by observation.

10. Interpret the knowledge and audience continuum.

11. Write informally about a key idea presented in this lesson.

TEXT ASSIGNMENT

Text: Gong and Dragga, *A Writer's Repertoire*, Chapter 1

Chapter 1 introduces key ideas that recur throughout the text. It gives a brief overview of the history of rhetoric and of James Kinneavy's theory of the aims of writing. You will need to read the chapter slowly and carefully because there is so much information in it, most of it likely to be new to you. You will probably want to return to this chapter as you work through the text to refresh your memory of some of the important terms and ideas. Remember, though, that these key ideas run like threads throughout the rest of the book. You will have ample opportunity to improve your understanding of the canons of rhetoric, the three appeals, the aims of writing, and all the other significant ideas in this rich chapter. Use the following questions to guide your reading:

1. What do the authors mean by the term *rhetoric*? How does their definition differ from popular use of the term, which often has negative connotations?

2. What is the relationship between the oral and written components of the "territory of rhetoric"?

3. What are the five canons of rhetoric? How has the use of the five canons changed from classical to contemporary times?

4. What are the appeals identified by Aristotle?

5. What are the key parts of the rhetorical situation? How are they related to each other?

6. What is meant by the communication triangle?

7. What are the aims of writing, according to Kinneavy's theory?

8. How are the aims related to the communication triangle?

VIDEO ASSIGNMENT

Video: "Rhetorical Heritage, Modern Applications"

"Rhetorical Heritage, Modern Applications" briefly surveys the history of rhetoric as a field of study, defines the five canons of rhetoric as they were practiced in classical times and as they are used today, and introduces the theories of James Kinneavy. In the program, you will meet distinguished scholars and teachers of rhetoric who will share their knowledge of and enthusiasm for the study of rhetoric. Following is a brief description of what you will see and questions to guide your viewing:

1. A brief documentary in which three scholars of rhetoric tell about major events and figures in the history of rhetoric:

   • When and where did rhetoric begin? Why was it necessary?

   • How did Plato and Aristotle differ in their views of rhetoric?

   • What role did rhetoric play in medieval education?

- How did the arrival of the printing press in the fifteenth century change the course of rhetoric?

- Why did the study of rhetoric decline in the last century? Why is it being revived today?

- According to the expert, how has the field of rhetoric changed?

2. An interview with Dr. Gwendolyn Gong, one of the authors of the text, in which she defines the five canons of rhetoric as they were used in ancient times and as they are used now:

- What is invention? How are the appeals (*ethos*, *pathos*, and *logos*) related to invention?

- What is arrangement?

- What is style?

- According to the expert, are the canons the definitive word on rhetoric?

3. An interview with Dr. James Kinneavy in which he explains his theory of the aims of writing:

- What are the four aims of writing? What examples of each does Dr. Kinneavy give?

- How are the aims related to the communication triangle?

- What are some examples of the aims of writing that students might encounter in college, according to the expert?

Lesson 2

The Psychology of Writing

LESSON ASSIGNMENT

Review the following assignment in order to schedule your time appropriately. Pay careful attention; the titles and numbers of the textbook chapter, the study guide lesson, and the video program may be different from one another.

Text:
    Gong and Dragga, *A Writer's Repertoire*,
    Read Chapter 2, "Composing Process," pp. 37–53.

Handbook:
    Hairston and Ruszkiewicz, *The Scott, Foresman Handbook for Writers*,
    Refer to all sections in the following chapters:
        Chapters 2, 3, and 4

Video:
    View "The Psychology of Writing"
    from the series, *A Writer's Exchange*.

OVERVIEW

In "The Psychology of Writing" you will find out what researchers have learned in the past twenty years about how people write. You will find out how to apply this current research to your own writing process so that you develop a process that is right for you. You will find out how to turn your ideas into writing that communicates to your readers exactly what you want to say. Finally, you will learn how your own thoughts and feelings as well as circumstances in your life affect your writing and how you can control some of these internal and external influences. When you have finished this lesson, you will have an increased understanding of the psychological processes involved in writing, some ideas about improving your own writing process, and a better grasp of strategies for dealing with the psychological and social influences on your own writing. You should be able to write a brief, informal description of your own writing process.

LEARNING OBJECTIVES

Goal

You should be able to summarize the research of the past twenty years on the psychological and cognitive processes involved in writing and relate current cognitive models of this process to the classical canons of rhetoric, and understand internal and external psychological and social influences on the writing process.

Objectives

Upon completing this lesson, you should be able to:

1. Explain the "recursive" nature of writing processes.

2. Relate current psychological/social descriptions of composing processes to the classical divisions of rhetoric.

3. Describe the processes of planning, translating, and reviewing.

4. Contrast the characteristics of writer-based and reader-based prose and explain their close relationship.

5. List and explain common internal and external influences on composing.

6. Write an informal description of your own writing process.

TEXT ASSIGNMENT

Text: Gong and Dragga, *A Writer's Repertoire*, Chapter 2

Chapter 2 summarizes the research of the past twenty years on the psychological and cognitive processes involved in writing and relates current ideas about the writing process to the classical canons of rhetoric. It also discusses internal and external influences on the writing process. This chapter is packed with useful information of a general nature: the purpose of the chapter is not to teach you how to write a particular paper, but rather to give you some insights into your own composing process so that you can improve it. You may need to refer to Chapter 1 when you get to the section on the composing process and the classical canons. Use the following questions to guide your reading:

1. What is meant by the "recursive" nature of the writing process?

2. How do the current descriptions of the writing process relate to the classical canons described in Chapter 1?

3. What are the processes of planning, translating, and reviewing?

4. What are some common internal and external influences on composing?

VIDEO ASSIGNMENT

Video: "The Psychology of Writing"

"The Psychology of Writing" illustrates current research on how people write and what factors influence a person's writing. You will also learn how to translate your ideas from writing just for yourself to writing appropriately for an audience. Following is a brief description of what you will see and questions to guide your viewing:

1. Interviews with accomplished writers, including a lawyer, a college professor, and a professional writer, that illustrate the recursive nature of the composing process:

   • Each writer's process is slightly different from the others. How does the expert respond to these differences?

   • Do the writers move through a stage-by-stage process when they write or do they mix up the processes (such as *invention, drafting,* and *revision*) as they write?

   • What new research does the expert cite about the composing process?

2. A scenario showing how a student revises a letter to a prospective employer from a writer-based piece to a reader-based one:

   • What is the problem with the student's first version of the letter?

   • How do the revisions make the letter better?

   • What is the difference between writer-based and reader-based writing? Refer to the student's letter as an example.

   • What is the expert's view of writer-based writing?

3. Interviews with students illustrating the concept of internal and external influences on the writer:

   • How do these students handle their external influences?

   • How do they handle the internal influences on their writing?

   • What tips does the expert offer to deal with these influences?

Lesson 3

Writing with an Expressive Aim

LESSON ASSIGNMENT

Review the following assignment in order to schedule your time appropriately. Pay careful attention; the titles and numbers of the textbook chapter, the study guide lesson, and the video program may be different from one another.

Text:
> Gong and Dragga, *A Writer's Repertoire*,
> Read Chapter 8, "Expressive Aim Writing: An Overview,"
> > pp. 214–265.

Handbook:
> Hairston and Ruszkiewicz, *The Scott, Foresman Handbook for Writers*,
> Refer to the sections dealing with the following topics:
> > Chapter 1—purpose
> > Chapter 2—organization
> > Chapter 7—paragraph patterns, transitions and parallelism, paragraph appearance
> > Chapter 8—opening paragraphs

Video:
> View "Writing with an Expressive Aim"
> from the series, *A Writer's Exchange*.

OVERVIEW

In "Writing with an Expressive Aim: An Overview," you will be introduced to one of the aims of writing that you will often use in your college and personal writing, the expressive. In this lesson, you will learn what the expressive aim is, when you can expect to use it in academic and personal writing, and how to write an expressive paper.

As you write an expressive aim essay, you will wish to return to this lesson because the video and text have many suggestions to help you.

After you have finished the lesson, you should know what expressive aim writing is and what its main purposes are. Although you will need to practice expressive aim writing, when you finish this lesson you should be able to explain narrative and descriptive techniques often used in expressive aim writing.

LEARNING OBJECTIVES

Goal

You should be able to define the expressive aim, illustrate commonly used techniques for achieving that aim using knowledge by participation and knowledge by observation, recognize common types of expressive aim writing, and read and respond to expressive aim writing.

Objectives

Upon completing this lesson, you should be able to:

1. Define expressive aim writing.

2. Identify characteristics of expressive aim writing.

3. Describe the assessment and mapping of a piece of expressive aim writing.

4. Illustrate the importance of establishing the writer's credibility.

5. Identify narrative techniques in expressive aim writing.

6. Explain the importance of description as a technique in expressive aim writing.

7. Identify descriptive techniques such as the use of dialogue, details, and setting to describe a person or place.

8. Explain the importance of realizing and communicating the significance of the writer's personal experience.

9. Analyze rhetorical techniques in a piece of expressive aim writing.

10. Map a piece of expressive aim writing on the audience and knowledge continua.

11. Write an informal response to a piece of expressive aim writing.

TEXT ASSIGNMENT

Text: Gong and Dragga, *A Writer's Repertoire*, Chapter 8

Chapter 8 introduces you to the major purposes of expressive aim writing: narration and description. The information in the chapter applies to all expressive aim writing. You will need to refer to this chapter again when you begin to write an expressive aim paper. For now, try to grasp what expressive aim writing is and how you can begin to write expressively. Use the following to guide your reading:

1. Define expressive aim writing.

2. List three purposes of expressive aim writing.

3. How does Tamikka's map of her rhetorical situation (pp. 247-249) illustrate her knowledge of her subject and her understanding of her audience?

4. How can a student writer establish credibility in an expressive paper?

5. How can narrative action, narrative organization, and point of view be used to tell the story of an incident that had an impact on the writer?

6. How can descriptive details, dialogue, and setting be used to describe a character?

7. Why is it important to realize and to communicate the significance of your own personal experience in an expressive paper?

VIDEO ASSIGNMENT

Video: "Writing with an Expressive Aim"

"Writing with an Expressive Aim" is a general introduction to the topic. It explains what expressive aim writing is, when you might use it, and how to write it effectively. Following is a brief description of what you will see and questions to guide your viewing:

1. A woman who has used expressive writing to understand herself better as well as to communicate with others:

   • How does the story illustrate the characteristics of expressive aim writing?

   • How would you assess and map her story?

   • What insights does the expert offer on the value of journals?

2. A scenario in which a concerned parent uses expressive writing to address a significant educational issue:

   • How does the parent establish credibility in his letter?

   • How does the parent communicate the significance of his experience with violence in the school to the reader?

- What improvements does the expert suggest for the parent's letter?

3. An interview with a newspaper columnist who shares the various narrative techniques he uses:

   - What are the sources of inspiration for the columnist?

   - What narrative techniques does the columnist illustrate?

   - What does the expert think a student writer can learn from the columnist about expressive writing?

5. A scenario in which a student struggles with common problems of expressive writing, but gets help from a professor and fellow student:

   - What problem does his friend Michelle point out in Dion's descriptive paper?

   - What suggestions does the professor make to Dion about his second draft?

   - What suggestions does the expert make to improve Dion's paper?

   - What tips does the expert give for writing description?

RELATED ACTIVITIES

These activities are not required unless your instructor assigns them. They are offered as suggestions to help you learn more about the material presented in this lesson.

Text: Gong and Dragga, *A Writer's Repertoire*, Part VI, "Readings,"
    "So Tsi-fai," pp. 508–511,
    "Herman Hollerith: Inventor, Manager, Entrepreneur—A
        Centennial Remembrance," pp. 511–526,
    "Coretta King: Revisited," pp. 526–534,
    "Wyoming: The Solace of Open Spaces," pp. 534–543.

The readings are written by experienced writers in a range of fields. The essays relate specifically to this lesson; these essays are examples of the type of writing discussed in the text and on the video. They are professional examples of writing with the same aim that you will be using for your own paper. Your instructor may ask you to read one or more of the essays, or you may wish to read one or more of the essays on your own. If so, the questions at the end of the selections will help you analyze the essays.

Lesson 4

Writing Narration

LESSON ASSIGNMENT

Review the following assignment in order to schedule your time appropriately. Pay careful attention; the titles and numbers of the textbook chapter, the study guide lesson, and the video program may be different from one another.

Text:
> Gong and Dragga, *A Writer's Repertoire*,
> Review Chapter 8, "Expressive Aim Writing: An Overview,"
>   pp. 252–256,
> Read Chapter 9, "Repertoire Focus: Recounting Events,"
>   pp. 267–293.

Handbook:
> Hairston and Ruszkiewicz, *The Scott, Foresman Handbook for Writers*,
> Refer to the sections dealing with the following topics:
>   Chapter 2—narrative design
>   Chapter 7—narration paragraph patterns
>   Chapter 8—opening paragraphs

Video:
> View "Writing Narration"
> from the series, *A Writer's Exchange*.

OVERVIEW

"Writing Narration" prepares you to write a paper that recounts an event that is important in your life. You will learn how to make such an event meaningful to readers whether you participated in the event personally or learned about it through reading or talking with other people. You will learn writing techniques that will make the event come alive for your readers: selecting just the right details, dramatizing the event through dialogue, sequencing the events so that readers can easily follow your story, and presenting the event from a consistent point of view so that readers are not confused. Although you will be using these skills in a narrative essay, you will see how the writing skills you learn in this lesson can be used in other writing that you will do in college and in the work world.

When you have completed the lesson, you should be able to explain what narration is and how it is used in expressive aim writing, read and respond to narrative pieces by both student and professional writers, and write your own narrative essay using the specific skills taught in the lesson.

LEARNING OBJECTIVES

Goal

You should be able to write a paper using effective narration to achieve an expressive aim.

Objectives

Upon completing this lesson, you should be able to:

1. Differentiate between narration for a referential or persuasive aim and narration for an expressive aim.

2. Differentiate between simple storytelling and narration with a specific expressive purpose.

3. Explain the use of narrative techniques such as action, point of view, and narrative organization, including variations of the chronological sequence of arrangement often used in narrative writing.

4. Recognize examples of narrative writing in print.

5. Cite uses of narrative writing for an expressive purpose in your academic and personal worlds.

6. Explain or diagram the rhetorical situation of narrative writing.

7. Read examples of narration critically.

8. Respond to written examples (professional and/or student) of narrative writing.

9. Write a draft of a paper with an expressive aim using narration, using knowledge from participation, observation, or both.

TEXT ASSIGNMENT

Text: Gong and Dragga, *A Writer's Repertoire*, Chapter 8

Chapter 8 introduces the general concepts of writing for an expressive aim. The whole chapter gives useful background information, but pp. 252-256 apply specifically to writing narration. A review of these pages will be helpful to you in reading a narrative essay and, especially, if you are writing a narrative essay. The following questions should guide your review:

1. What is the difference between narration for a referential or persuasive aim and narration for an expressive aim?

2. What is the difference between simply telling a story and using narrative with a specific expressive purpose?

3. How can the following techniques be used to make a narrative essay effective?
   - action
   - point of view
   - chronological sequence of arrangement

Text: Gong and Dragga, *A Writer's Repertoire*, Chapter 9

Chapter 9, "Narration," is very different in purpose from Chapter 8. In this chapter, you will find examples of narrative papers that other students have written. These essays are not perfect, but they are good examples of essays produced by college freshmen in response to the topic you are working on. Use the questions at the end of each essay to focus your response to that essay. Then think about what you can learn from all the essays.

VIDEO ASSIGNMENT

Video: "Writing Narration"

"Writing Narration" focuses on specific writing techniques that will help you write a narrative essay. Following is a brief description of what you will see and questions to guide your viewing:

1. A scenario in which a writer tells the same story for different aims:

   • Alice tells the story of her near accident three times. Which version is referential? Which is persuasive? Which is expressive? What qualities distinguish the expressive example from the other two?

   • What comments does the expert have about writing narration?

2. An interview with a professional writer who shares some of her experiences in writing narration as well as some of her techniques:

   • How does the writer find topics to write about?

   • What suggestions are offered by the expert for finding a topic?

3. A scenario showing a student struggling to find and develop a narrative essay:

- How does the student find a topic?

- After selecting a topic, how does the student find information on it?

- What suggestions does the professor offer the student for improving his paper?

- What other narrative techniques does the expert suggest in addition to those used by the student?

RELATED ACTIVITY

This activity is not required unless your instructor assigns it. It is offered as a suggestion to help you learn more about the material presented in this lesson.

Text: Gong and Dragga, *A Writer's Repertoire*, Part VI, "Readings," "So Tsi-fai," pp. 508–511.

The reading is written by a graduate student, a more experienced writer than the authors of the essays in Chapter 9. Your instructor may ask you to read the essay, or you may wish to read the essay on your own. If so, the questions at the end of the selection will help you analyze the essay.

Lesson 5

Writing Description

LESSON ASSIGNMENT

Review the following assignment in order to schedule your time appropriately. Pay careful attention; the titles and numbers of the textbook chapter, the study guide lesson, and the video program may be different from one another.

Text:
> Gong and Dragga, *A Writer's Repertoire*,
> Review Chapter 8, "Expressive Aim Writing: An Overview,"
>   pp. 259 and 244,
> Read Chapter 10, "Repertoire Focus: Portraying Characters and
> Depicting Places," pp. 295–326.

Handbook:
> Hairston and Ruszkiewicz, *The Scott, Foresman Handbook for Writers*,
> Refer to the section dealing with the following topic:
>   Chapter 2—perspectives on thesis development

Video:
> View "Writing Description"
> from the series, *A Writer's Exchange*.

OVERVIEW

In "Writing Description," you will learn how to describe people and places so that your readers will understand their significance in your life. You will learn techniques that you can use in writing a descriptive essay and also in using description in other kinds of writing. You will learn specific techniques, such as the use of spatial arrangement, the use of dialogue, and the use of specific details to make your description clear to your reader.

When you have completed the lesson, you should be able to explain what description is and how it is used in expressive aim writing, read and respond to descriptive pieces by both student and professional writers, and write your own descriptive essay using the skills taught in the lesson.

LEARNING OBJECTIVES

Goal

You should be able to effectively describe characters and places in expressive writing.

Objectives

Upon completing this lesson, you should be able to:

1. Differentiate between description for a referential or persuasive aim and description for an expressive aim.

2. Describe common techniques for descriptive writing such as the use of spatial arrangement, dialogue, and specific details.

3. Recognize examples of descriptive writing for an expressive aim in print.

4. Cite uses of description for an expressive aim in the academic and personal worlds.

5. Explain or diagram the rhetorical situation of an assigned topic.

6. Read examples of descriptive writing critically.

7. Respond to written examples (professional and/or student) of descriptive writing for an expressive aim.

8. Write a draft of a paper with an expressive aim describing a person or place.

TEXT ASSIGNMENT

Text: Gong and Dragga, *A Writer's Repertoire*, Chapter 8

Chapter 8 introduces the general concepts of writing for an expressive aim. You may wish to review the whole chapter, but the section on techniques for descriptive writing (pp. 257-261) and the uses for descriptive writing (p. 244) will be especially useful. The following should guide your review:

1. What is the difference between description for a referential or persuasive aim and description for an expressive aim?

2. Describe the following techniques that are often used in descriptive writing: the use of spatial arrangement, the use of dialogue, and the use of specific details.

3. What are some examples of descriptive writing in the academic and personal worlds?

Text: Gong and Dragga, *A Writer's Repertoire*, Chapter 10

Chapter 10 gives you models of descriptive writing rather than information about it as Chapter 8 does. In Chapter 10, you will find student essays and their accompanying journals that will show you what your professor might expect from a good (but not perfect) student paper. Use the questions at the end of each essay to focus your response to that essay. Then think about what you can learn from all the essays.

VIDEO ASSIGNMENT

Video: "Writing Description"

"Writing Description" shows you how to begin writing a descriptive paper. You will see writers facing and solving the same problems you will face when you write a descriptive paper. Following is a brief description of what you will see and questions to guide your viewing:

1. A documentary about a writing coach and members of her writing group who discuss their strategies for writing description:

   - What techniques do the writing group participants use to make their descriptions of people vivid and interesting to their readers?

   - What writing exercise does the writing coach suggest for getting started on a description of a person?

   - What comments does the expert offer about the techniques discussed in the documentary?

2. An interview with a novelist on his techniques for describing a place:

   - Why does the novelist think the sense of place is so important?

   - How does the novelist convey a sense of place in his works?

   - According to the expert, what makes the description of the Rio Grande valley effective?

3. A documentary about students who write descriptions of people and places as part of an unusual English course:

   - What part does descriptive writing play in the students' work?

- How do the students use their journals in their more polished writings?

- What does the expert think other writers can learn from the experiences of these English students?

RELATED ACTIVITIES

These activities are not required unless your instructor assigns them. They are offered as suggestions to help you learn more about the material presented in this lesson.

Text: Gong and Dragga, *A Writer's Repertoire*, Part VI, "Readings,"
   "Herman Hollerith: Inventor, Manager, Entrepreneur—A
      Centennial Remembrance," pp. 511–526,
   "Coretta King: Revisited," pp. 526–534,
   "Wyoming: The Solace of Open Spaces," pp. 534–543.

The readings are written by skilled writers, one of them (Alice Walker) an acclaimed novelist and essayist. You will notice, though, that these writers use the same techniques you are learning in this lesson. Your instructor may assign you to read one or more of the essays, or you may wish to read one or more of the essays on your own. If so, the questions at the end of the selections will help you analyze the essays.

Lesson 6

Starting a Collaborative Writing Group

LESSON ASSIGNMENT

Review the following assignment in order to schedule your time appropriately. Pay careful attention; the titles and numbers of the textbook chapter, the study guide lesson, and the video program may be different from one another.

Text:
> Gong and Dragga, *A Writer's Repertoire*,
> Read Chapter 3, "Collaborative Writing," pp. 55-62
>   and pp. 74-75.

Handbook:
> Hairston and Ruszkiewicz, *The Scott, Foresman Handbook for Writers*,
> Refer to the section dealing with the following topic:
>   Chapter 3—draft collaboration

Video:
> View "Starting a Collaborative Writing Group"
> from the series, *A Writer's Exchange*.

OVERVIEW

"Starting a Collaborative Writing Group" introduces you to a skill practiced by experienced writers in the work world and encouraged by many professors in college courses: the ability to collaborate with other people to improve your own writing and to help others improve their writing. Most of the writing done at work is a team effort. Generally, a writer asks for input from colleagues and superiors before sending out a document. In this lesson, you will learn proven techniques for giving and receiving suggestions for improving your writing. You will learn how to phrase your suggestions so they are helpful and not offensive, what to look for in the writing of others, and how to incorporate useful suggestions into your own writing. These interpersonal skills will not only make you a better writer, but a better team member as well.

LEARNING OBJECTIVES

Goal

You should be able to collaborate with peers as well as with the instructor in producing text, respond to others' writing, integrate collaborative responses into a finished text, and understand sequential collaboration.

Objectives

Upon completing this lesson, you should be able to:

1. Differentiate between individual and collaborative writing.

2. Explain why the ability to collaborate with others in producing a text is a life skill as well as an academic skill.

3. Cite examples of collaborative communication (oral and written) in everyday life.

4. Explain why collaboration improves an individual's writing abilities as well as a specific text.

5. List a few guidelines for giving and accepting peer response to writing.

6. Respond to a text written by a classmate, following guidelines established in the lesson.

7. Revise your text, using responses from peers as suggestions for improvements.

TEXT ASSIGNMENT

Text: Gong and Dragga, *A Writer's Repertoire*, Chapter 3

The video will give you an introduction to the techniques for collaboration you need to know. The text chapter will serve primarily as a reference for you. You may want to skim the chapter as a whole, focusing on the sections "Individual Writing versus Collaborative Writing," "Two Orientations of Collaboration," "Your Experience with Collaboration," and "Collaboration and Individual Writing Abilities," and noting the guidelines for giving and accepting peer response on pp. 74-75. The questions below refer to these sections of the chapter only.

1. What is the difference between individual and collaborative writing?

2. Why is the ability to collaborate with others in producing a text a life skill as well as an academic skill?

3. What are some examples of collaborative communication (spoken and written) in everyday life?

4. Why does collaboration improve an individual's writing abilities?

5. What are some guidelines for giving and accepting peer response to a piece of writing?

VIDEO ASSIGNMENT

Video: "Starting a Collaborative Writing Group"

The video program gives you information on effective collaboration and models good collaboration for you. Following is a brief description of what you will see and questions to guide your viewing:

1. A documentary about members of a student writers' group and their use of collaboration:

   • What kinds of responses do the students make to each others' papers?

   • What do the students mean by reading with "soft eyes"?

   • How is collaboration beneficial to the students?

   • What comments does the expert make on the group's use of feedback ("soft eyes")?

2. A short documentary about members of a writers' group and their use of collaboration:

   • What benefits of collaboration are noted by the members of the writing group?

   • What does the expert suggest other writers can learn from this group?

3. A short documentary about two professional writers:

   • What role does technology play in the collaboration between the two professional writers?

   • According to the expert, how is collaboration at a distance different from face-to-face collaboration?

Lesson 7

Discovering Ideas: The Canon of Invention

LESSON ASSIGNMENT

Review the following assignment in order to schedule your time appropriately. Pay careful attention; the titles and numbers of the textbook chapter, the study guide lesson, and the video program may be different from one another.

Text:
> Gong and Dragga, *A Writer's Repertoire*,
> Read Chapter 4, "Invention," pp. 79–118.

Handbook:
> Hairston and Ruszkiewicz, *The Scott, Foresman Handbook for Writers*,
> Refer to the sections dealing with the following topics:
>> Chapter 2—topics, topic focus, thesis statement,
>>   thesis development
>> Chapter 32—topic selection, information location

Video:
> View "Discovering Ideas: The Canon of Invention"
> from the series, *A Writer's Exchange*.

OVERVIEW

If you've ever had "blank page paralysis" when writing a paper, you need the lesson on *invention*. In this lesson, you will learn tried-and-true techniques for getting started on a paper and for getting going again when you are stuck. "Discovering Ideas: The Canon of Invention" introduces the first of the five canons of classical rhetoric, but it also offers insights from contemporary psychology into the task of generating ideas for writing. In this lesson, you will learn many ways of finding ideas to write about. When you finish the lesson, you should be able to practice any one of several invention strategies, but more important, you will be able to determine which strategies work best for you.

LEARNING OBJECTIVES

Goal

You should be able to understand the first of the five canons of classical rhetoric, use insights from contemporary psychology in the task of generating ideas for writing, analyze audience from the classical, psychological, and social perspectives, and discover information through personal knowledge as well as through research.

Objectives

Upon completing this lesson, you should be able to:

1. Define invention both as a classical canon of rhetoric and as a part of the composing process.

2. Explain the relationship of invention to the rhetorical situation (the knowledge and audience continua).

3. Identify the aim and purpose of your own text.

4. Analyze the audience for your text from one of the perspectives presented (classical, cognitive, social).

5. Use one or more of the invention methods presented in the lesson (personal records, brainstorming, pentad, classical topics, and visualizing) to discover your knowledge of a subject.

6. Use one or more of the research methods presented (interviews, questionnaires, library research) to discover additional information on a topic.

7. Describe how knowledge by participation and knowledge by observation may be combined to generate a text.

8. Use one or more of the invention strategies explained in the lesson to generate a text.

TEXT ASSIGNMENT

Text: Gong and Dragga, *A Writer's Repertoire*, Chapter 4

Chapter 4 is a comprehensive treatment of invention strategies. It describes several ways of getting started and suggests exercises to help you practice these ways. You will want to read the entire chapter, but focus your reading on those strategies most appealing to you. Everyone develops a favorite way to get started. This lesson is an opportunity for you to try out some new ways and to hone in on those that seem to work best with your own writing processes. Use this chapter as a resource; choose what you use from it based on your own needs. Use the following to guide your reading:

1. What is invention? How does invention relate to the classical canons? How does it relate to the composing process?

2. How does invention relate to the rhetorical situation (the knowledge and audience continua)?

3. How do you identify the aim and purpose of your text?

4. What are the classical, cognitive, and social perspectives from which an audience may be analyzed?

5. Briefly describe the following invention strategies: personal records, brainstorming, the pentad, classical topics, and visualizing.

6. Briefly describe the following research methods for discovering additional information on a topic: interviews, library research, and questionnaires.

7. How can knowledge by participation and knowledge by observation be combined to generate a text?

VIDEO ASSIGNMENT

Video: "Discovering Ideas: The Canon of Invention"

"Discovering Ideas: The Canon of Invention" explains the classical canon of invention by showing how it relates to modern ideas of the writing process. You will see how successful writers use various invention strategies and how these strategies help them find ideas and create papers. Following is a brief description of what you will see and questions to guide your viewing:

1. A scenario in which a student in a college writing class selects a topic for a personal essay, uses brainstorming to clarify the topic, and relies on personal records to flesh out the essay:

   - How does the brainstorming session help the student focus on the topic?

   - How does the journal help the student develop the topic?

   - Why does the expert think the brainstorming session and journal entries are helpful to the student?

2. A scenario in which a student uses computer software and mapping to develop a topic:

   - How does computer software help the student develop a topic?

   - What is the difference between the invention strategies in the computer software and mapping, according to the professor?

   - What is the value of invention techniques, according to the expert?

- How does the expert advise inexperienced writers to decide what invention strategy to use?

3. An interview with a business executive who uses both personal experience and research to produce business documents:

  - How do the executive and his staff gather information to use in various documents?

  - Why is it necessary to go beyond the personal knowledge of the staff to produce proposals and detailed itineraries?

  - According to the expert, how does research fit into the invention process?

Lesson 8

Organizing Ideas: The Canon of Arrangement

LESSON ASSIGNMENT

Review the following assignment in order to schedule your time appropriately. Pay careful attention; the titles and numbers of the textbook chapter, the study guide lesson, and the video program may be different from one another.

Text:
> Gong and Dragga, *A Writer's Repertoire*,
> Read Chapter 5, "Arrangement," pp. 119–162.

Handbook:
> Hairston and Ruszkiewicz, *The Scott, Foresman Handbook for Writers*,
> Refer to the sections dealing with the following topics:
>> Chapter 2—topics, organization, titles
> Refer to all sections in the following chapters:
>> Chapters 7 and 8

Video:
> View "Organizing Ideas: The Canon of Arrangement"
> from the series, *A Writer's Exchange*.

OVERVIEW

In approaching a writing task, you may find that arranging your ideas in a way that communicates what you want to say and that readers can readily understand presents great challenges. How can you put your ideas in an order that is logical, but also clear to the reader? What do you do if your readers expect a particular arrangement of material? How can you help your readers understand your main points?

"Organizing Ideas: The Canon of Arrangement" will give you some answers to these and other common questions about the organization of ideas into a coherent paper. *Arrangement* is the second of the five classical canons.

In ancient times, of course, the term referred to the arrangement of arguments in an oration; today we use the term to refer to the organizational principles that help readers understand what the writer wants to communicate. In this lesson, we will show you that arranging material effectively is a skill that can help both writer and reader communicate. You will not learn a specific pattern of arrangement, such as the *five-paragraph theme* or the *five-part argument*. Instead, we will focus on the rationale for paying attention to arrangement by showing how successful writers cope with the problems of arrangement they face in a variety of writing tasks. You will learn the three key qualities of good arrangement, *unity, development,* and *cohesion.* You will also learn how to achieve these qualities in your own writing.

When you have finished the lesson, you will not have a magic formula to use in all your writing for the rest of your life. But you will understand why arrangement is an important aspect of writing and how to approach the task of arranging your ideas for a paper.

LEARNING OBJECTIVES

Goal

You should be able to use the second of the five canons of classical rhetoric, arrangement, for organizing text and understand traditional concepts of organization such as the rhetorical modes, the *outline*, and the *thesis statement*, as well as newer methods of developing ideas such as the use of *discourse blocs*.

Objectives

Upon completing this lesson, you should be able to:

1. Define arrangement both as a classical canon of rhetoric and as a part of the composing process.

2. Explain how appropriate arrangement of ideas in a text is helpful both to readers and to the writer.

3. Evaluate the sufficiency and relevance of research to achieve a specific rhetorical purpose.

4. Define and write an appropriate thesis statement.

5. Differentiate between explicit and implicit thesis statements.

6. List two characteristics of effective thesis statements.

7. Differentiate between sequential and categorical principles of organization.

8. Explain the relationship between discourse blocs and the development of ideas in a text.

9. Demonstrate the relationship between discourse blocs and paragraphs.

10. List and explain several methods of development for discourse blocs (the rhetorical modes).

11. List and explain the functions of key types of discourse blocs: titles, introductions, transitional discourse blocs, and conclusions.

12. Identify common problems with organization in your own writing and in peers' papers: divided thesis, writer-based arrangement, unfocused or underdeveloped writing.

13. Identify trouble-shooting strategies for common problems with organization.

14. Define the term *coherence* and explain how coherence may be achieved by using repetition, substitution, and transitions.

15. Explain how an outline may be used to preview or to review ideas in a text.

16. List the conventions for outlines.

17. Use one or more of the strategies for arrangement to organize or to revise a text.

TEXT ASSIGNMENT

Text: Gong and Dragga, *A Writer's Repertoire*, Chapter 5

The chapter on arrangement is broad in scope and deep in detail. It is a chapter to be read more than once and to be used often as a reference. The chapter explains what arrangement is, why it is important to use an effective arrangement, and how to do so. Furthermore, the chapter also gives direct instruction in avoiding the most common problems with arrangement. You will want to read the whole chapter first, using the points below to focus your reading. Later, you will want to return to those sections of the chapter that meet your own needs as a writer. For instance, the section on avoiding common pitfalls in arrangement will not apply equally to all writers. If you do not have a particular problem with arrangement, you need not pore over the section that explains how to avoid it. On the other hand, if your professor suggests that you need some work on, say, development, it would be wise to read that section carefully and more than once. Because this chapter is based on current research, you may find some information and terminology that is unfamiliar. Use the following to guide your reading:

1. How is arrangement both a classical canon of rhetoric and a part of the composing process?

2. How is the appropriate arrangement of ideas in a text helpful both to readers and to the writer?

3. How can you evaluate the sufficiency and relevance of research to achieve a specific rhetorical purpose?

4. What is a thesis statement? What is the difference between an explicit and an implicit thesis statement? What makes a thesis statement effective?

5. What is the difference between sequential and categorical principles of organization?

6. What is the difference between discourse blocs and paragraphs? How are discourse blocs related to ideas in a text?

7. What are the functions of the following key types of discourse blocs: titles, introductions, transitions, and conclusions?

8. Explain the following common problems with organization, and identify a trouble-shooting strategy for each: divided thesis, writer-based arrangement, and unfocused or underdeveloped writing.

9. What is coherence in writing? How can it be achieved?

10. How can an outline be used to preview or to review ideas in a text? What are the major conventions for outlines?

VIDEO ASSIGNMENT

Video: "Organizing Ideas: The Canon of Arrangement"

"Organizing Ideas: The Canon of Arrangement" explains the three qualities that make a piece of writing clear and understandable to the reader: development, unity, and cohesion. You will see how experienced writers achieve these qualities and how you, too, can write coherent, clear papers. Following is a brief description of what you will see and questions to guide your viewing:

1. A famous orator's speech and an expert analysis of it:

   • Could you easily follow the speaker's ideas?

- Why does the expert say the speech is effective?

2. An interview with a speech writer who uses a thesis statement to unify one of his speeches:

   - Why does the writer use a thesis sentence in the speech discussed?

   - What organizational pattern does the writer use and why?

   - What suggestions does the expert give for writing a clear thesis statement?

3. An interview with a student who explains how to make the key parts of a paper flow logically:

   - How would you describe the approach to writing the various segments of the paper (introduction, conclusion, and paragraph blocs) taken by the student?

   - What suggestions does the expert have on organizing and developing topics?

4. An interview with a business person who explains how to achieve cohesion in a paper:

   - What devices does the writer use to link ideas together in the essay?

   - What suggestions does the expert offer for gaining cohesion?

Lesson 9

Writing with an Informative Aim

LESSON ASSIGNMENT

Review the following assignment in order to schedule your time appropriately. Pay careful attention; the titles and numbers of the textbook chapter, the study guide lesson, and the video program may be different from one another.

Text:

Gong and Dragga, *A Writer's Repertoire*,
Read Chapter 11, "Referential Aim Writing: An Overview,"
   pp. 329–346.

Handbook:

Hairston and Ruszkiewicz, *The Scott, Foresman Handbook for Writers*,
Refer to the section dealing with the following topic:
   Chapter 1—audience
Refer to all sections in the following chapters:
   Chapter 5, 32, and 33

Video:

View "Writing with an Informative Aim"
from the series, *A Writer's Exchange*.

OVERVIEW

In "Writing with an Informative Aim," you will be introduced to the kind of writing you will encounter most often in your studies and in the work world: writing that communicates information and explains a topic. You will learn what the special characteristics of this kind of writing are and how to incorporate them effectively into your own writing. When you finish this lesson, you will have the information you need to tackle a writing assignment with a referential aim.

LEARNING OBJECTIVES

Goal

You should be able to communicate information and explain a topic, to recognize the characteristics of referential aim writing, to write with this aim, and to analyze and respond to a text with this aim.

Objectives

Upon completing this lesson, you should be able to:

1. Relate referential aim writing to the communication triangle.

2. Define referential aim writing.

3. Cite examples of referential aim writing.

4. Describe the assessment and mapping of referential aim writing.

5. List and explain the most common purposes of referential aim writing, to explain and to analyze.

6. Explain the need for flexibility in integrating subordinate purposes into referential aim writing.

7. Analyze the referential rhetorical situation.

8. Develop and clarify a thesis for a referential aim paper.

9. Research and discover information to establish credibility, develop and refine a thesis, and communicate with an audience.

10. Evaluate information to support a thesis for a referential aim paper.

11. Respond to a text with a referential aim.

TEXT ASSIGNMENT

Text: Gong and Dragga, *A Writer's Repertoire*, Chapter 11

Chapter 11 gives you the information about referential aim writing that you will need to write a referential paper or to read referential writing critically. The chapter is full of information; you will want to read it carefully now, but you will also want to refer to it when you write a referential paper. The following questions will guide your reading:

1. What part of the communication triangle is emphasized in referential aim writing?

2. What is referential aim writing?

3. What are some examples of referential aim writing?

4. How can a writer use the knowledge and audience continua to describe the rhetorical situation of referential aim writing?

5. What are the two most common purposes of referential aim writing? How are they different from each other?

6. Why must the writer be flexible in incorporating subordinate aims into referential aim writing?

7. What are some suggestions for developing and clarifying a thesis for a referential paper?

8. What are some suggestions for gaining credibility in a referential paper?

9. What are some suggestions for communicating with an audience in a referential paper?

10. How can the writer decide which information to include in a referential paper and which to leave out?

VIDEO ASSIGNMENT

Video: "Writing with an Informative Aim"

"Writing with an Informative Aim" gives an overview of referential aim writing. You will learn what it is, where it is used in everyday life, and how to approach a referential writing task. Following is a brief description of what you will see and questions to guide your viewing:

1. A scenario showing the prevalence of referential aim writing in our lives:

   - How is the referential aim used in personal, business, and academic writing?

   - What distinction does the expert make between writing that analyzes and writing that explains?

   - What suggestions does the expert offer for getting ideas for referential writing?

2. A documentary about sociology students who explain how they developed a thesis for an informative paper:

   - Why does the professor assign papers calling for analysis?

   - What resources do the students use to come up with a thesis?

   - What does the expert think we can learn from the experiences of these students?

3. An interview with a journalist who describes how she writes for a referential aim:

   - How does the journalist choose which details to use and which to leave out?

   - How does the journalist's audience affect her writing?

- Does the journalist ever have a subordinate aim when she writes a referential piece for her newspaper?

- What suggestions does the expert have for establishing credibility in a referential piece?

- What does the expert say about the journalist's relationship to her audience?

RELATED ACTIVITIES

These activities are not required unless your instructor assigns them. They are offered as suggestions to help you learn more about the material presented in this lesson.

Text: Gong and Dragga, *A Writer's Repertoire*, Part VI, "Readings,"
    "Toward Something American," pp. 543–547,
    "Television Commercials and Food Orientation Among Teenagers
        in Puerto Rico," pp. 547–556,
    "Producing a Video on a Technical Subject: a Guide," pp. 557–575,
    "Teaching Maya Angelou's *I Know Why the Caged Bird Sings*: A
        Thematic Approach," pp. 575–582.

The readings are written by experienced writers in a range of fields. The essays relate specifically to this lesson; these essays are examples of the type of writing discussed in the text and on the video. They are professional examples of writing with the same aim that you will be using for your own paper. Your instructor may ask you to read one or more of the essays, or you may wish to read one or more of the essays on your own. If so, the questions at the end of the selections will help you analyze the essays.

Lesson 10

Introducing Explanatory Writing

LESSON ASSIGNMENT

Review the following assignment in order to schedule your time appropriately. Pay careful attention; the titles and numbers of the textbook chapter, the study guide lesson, and the video program may be different from one another.

Text:
>   Gong and Dragga, *A Writer's Repertoire*,
>   Review Chapter 11, "Referential Aim Writing: An Overview,"
>   pp. 336–346,
>   Read Chapter 12, "Repertoire Focus: Explaining a Subject,"
>   pp. 347–368.

Handbook:
>   Hairston and Ruszkiewicz, *The Scott, Foresman Handbook for Writers,*
>   Refer to the section dealing with the following topic:
>   Chapter 1—kinds of writing
>   Refer to all sections in the following chapters:
>   Chapters 5, 32, and 33

Video:
>   View "Introducing Explanatory Writing"
>   from the series, *A Writer's Exchange*.

OVERVIEW

In "Introducing Explanatory Writing," you will be introduced to a kind of writing that you will often encounter both as a reader and as a writer: writing that explains. This lesson is designed to launch you into a writing task requiring explanation; the lesson provides you with the information you need to write a draft on an explanatory paper. You will also learn how pervasive explanatory writing is in our lives and how important it is to us. You will learn how to choose a topic for an explanatory paper, gather information on the topic, and gear your paper for a specific audience. When you have finished the lesson, you should have a clear idea of what explanatory writing is and how to begin to develop an explanatory paper.

LEARNING OBJECTIVES

Goal

You should be able to employ one of the major uses of referential aim writing, explaining a topic, with an understanding of both the process and the product.

Objectives

Upon completing this lesson, you should be able to:

1. Define explanation as a means of achieving a referential aim in writing.

2. Describe methods for establishing credibility in an explanatory paper.

3. Explain how to develop and clarify a thesis for a paper of explanation.

4. List guidelines for locating and evaluating information to support a thesis for a paper of explanation.

5. List and explain at least two devices for motivating the audience for a piece of explanatory writing.

6. Cite uses of explanatory writing in the academic, personal, and work worlds.

7. Explain or diagram the rhetorical situation for an assigned task.

8. Read examples of explanatory writing analytically and critically.

9. Respond analytically to written examples (professional and/or student) of referential aim writing with an explanatory purpose.

TEXT ASSIGNMENT

Text: Gong and Dragga, *A Writer's Repertoire*, Chapter 11

Chapter 11 introduces the general concept of writing for a referential aim. The sections on establishing credibility in an explanatory paper (p. 336), developing and clarifying a thesis for an explanatory paper (pp. 338-341), locating and evaluating information to support a thesis for an explanatory paper (pp. 341-342), and motivating an audience in informative writing (pp. 342-344) are especially helpful. You may wish to review these sections before beginning to write an explanatory paper. The following should guide your review:

1. Describe methods for establishing credibility in an explanatory paper.

2. How do you develop and clarify a thesis for a paper of explanation?

3. What are some guidelines for locating and evaluating information to support a thesis for a paper of explanation?

4. What are two devices for motivating the audience of a paper of explanation?

Text: Gong and Dragga, *A Writer's Repertoire*, Chapter 12

Chapter 12, "Explaining a Subject," contains papers written by students using explanation as well as journal entries that show how they went about their writing tasks. Read the papers as examples of other students' work rather than as perfect models. Use the questions at the end of each essay to focus your response to that essay. Then think about what you can learn from all the essays.

VIDEO ASSIGNMENT

Video: "Introducing Explanatory Writing"

"Introducing Explanatory Writing" gives a brief overview of the uses of explanatory writing, then shows you how to get started writing a paper of explanation. Following is a brief description of what you will see and questions to guide your viewing:

1. Brief interviews illustrating the prevalence of explanatory writing in our personal, work, and academic worlds:

   - What characteristics do the information packet for new employees, the neighborhood newsletter, and the college catalog have in common?

   - What similarities among the three examples does the expert comment on?

2. A scenario of a history student researching a topic for an explanatory paper, and finding and evaluating sources for the paper:

   - What problems does the student encounter in finding an appropriate topic and developing a thesis for the paper? How are the problems solved?

   - Who is the audience for the student's paper?

   - How does the student choose material to appeal to the particular audience that the paper must address?

   - How does the student attempt to gain credibility in the paper?

- What advice does the expert offer about gaining credibility in explanatory papers?

- What advice does the expert offer students who get conflicting opinions about their papers?

3. An interview with the owner of an environmental consulting firm who regularly writes informatively for her clients:

   - What techniques does the consultant use to make her technical reports comprehensible to her readers?

   - How does she establish credibility?

   - How does the firm go about producing a single document with several contributors?

   - What does the expert say we can learn from the consultant about organizing material and using language to make a document easier to understand?

RELATED ACTIVITIES

These activities are not required unless your instructor assigns them. They are offered as suggestions to help you learn more about the material presented in this lesson.

Text: Gong and Dragga, *A Writer's Repertoire*, Part VI, "Readings,"
   "Toward Something American," pp. 543–547,
   "Producing a Video on a Technical Subject: A Guide," pp. 557–575.

The readings are written by more experienced writers than the students who wrote the essays in Chapter 12. You will notice, though, that these writers use the same techniques you are learning in this lesson. Your instructor may ask you to read one or more of the essays, or you may wish to read one or more of the essays on your own. If so, the questions at the end of the selections will help you analyze the essays.

Lesson 11

Writing an Explanatory Paper

LESSON ASSIGNMENT

Review the following assignment in order to schedule your time appropriately. Pay careful attention; the titles and numbers of the textbook chapter, the study guide lesson, and the video program may be different from one another.

Text:
    Gong and Dragga, *A Writer's Repertoire*,
    Review Chapter 11, "Referential Aim Writing: An Overview,"
        pp. 336-346,
    Review Chapter 12, "Repertoire Focus: Explaining a Subject,"
        pp. 347–368.

Handbook:
    Hairston and Ruszkiewicz, *The Scott, Foresman Handbook for Writers*,
    Refer to the section dealing with the following topic:
        Chapter 1—kinds of writing
    Refer to all sections in the following chapters:
        Chapters 5, 32, and 33

Video:
    View "Writing an Explanatory Paper"
    from the series, *A Writer's Exchange*.

OVERVIEW

In "Writing an Explanatory Paper," you will find out that explanatory writing can be complex and thus poses challenges both to the reader and to the writer. The lesson shows you how to meet these challenges by reading explanatory material critically and by writing your own explanations so that your readers can understand even difficult material. This lesson will help you solve some of the most common problems associated with explanatory writing: developing a clear thesis, deciding which supporting information to put in and which to leave out, and making connections with your audience. You will see explanatory writing used in personal, work, and academic settings.

When you have finished the lesson, you should be able to read explanatory writing more critically and write an explanatory essay that informs your readers about a subject that interests you.

LEARNING OBJECTIVES

Goal

You should be able to use explanation in your writing, evaluate explanatory texts in both academic and work contexts, draft your own explanatory essay, and respond analytically to other students' texts.

Objectives

Upon completing this lesson, you should be able to:

1. Establish credibility in an explanatory paper.

2. Develop and clarify a thesis for a paper of explanation.

3. Locate and evaluate information to support a thesis for a paper of explanation.

4. Use rhetorical techniques to motivate the audience for a piece of explanatory writing.

5. Cite applications of explanatory writing in the academic and work worlds.

6. Explain or diagram the rhetorical situation for an assigned task of referential writing with an explanatory purpose.

7. Read examples of explanatory writing analytically and critically.

8. Respond analytically to student writings using explanation for a referential aim.

9. Write a draft of a paper with a referential aim and an explanatory purpose, using knowledge by participation, observation, or a combination.

TEXT ASSIGNMENT

Text: Gong and Dragga, *A Writer's Repertoire*, Chapter 11

Chapter 11 introduces the general concepts of writing for a referential aim. The sections on establishing credibility in an informative paper (p. 336), developing and clarifying a thesis for an explanatory paper (pp. 338-341), and motivating an audience in informative writing (pp. 342-344) are especially helpful. You may wish to review these sections before beginning to write an explanatory paper. The following should guide your review:

1. Describe methods for establishing credibility in an explanatory paper.

2. How do you develop and clarify a thesis for a paper of explanation?

3. What are some guidelines for locating and evaluating information to support a thesis for a paper of explanation?

4. What are two devices for motivating the audience of a paper of explanation?

Text: Gong and Dragga, *A Writer's Repertoire*, Chapter 12,

Chapter 12, "Explaining a Subject," contains papers written by students using explanation as well as journal entries that show how they went about their writing tasks. Read the papers as examples of other students' work rather than as perfect models. Use the questions at the end of each essay to focus your response to that essay. Then think about what you can learn from all the essays.

VIDEO ASSIGNMENT

Video: "Writing an Explanatory Paper"

"Writing an Explanatory Paper" illustrates the complexity of some explanatory writing with situations from everyday life, work, and college. You will learn how to solve some of the most common problems in reading and writing explanations. Following is a brief description of what you will see and questions to guide your viewing:

1. An interview with a document design expert about the comparative effectiveness of two documents:

    - What are the differences between the explanation of lead in paint and the notice to borrowers?

    - What suggestions does the document design expert have for making a technical document readable?

    - What suggestions does the expert offer to readers for getting the information they need out of an explanatory document?

    - How does the expert suggest the writer of an explanatory piece motivate the audience, especially if the subject is a difficult one?

2. An interview with a public relations coordinator for a major hospital who writes explanatory pieces for a variety of audiences:

    - How does the public relations coordinator fit information to different audiences? Does she give all the audiences the same information?

- What comments does the expert have on selecting information to meet the needs of different audiences?

3. An interview with a geology student who must combine first-hand research with knowledge gained from books for a master's thesis:

  - Why does the graduate student need to include a review of the research in the field as well as his own findings in the paper?

  - What suggestions does the expert have for writing for an academic audience?

RELATED ACTIVITIES

These activities are not required unless your instructor assigns them. They are offered as suggestions to help you learn more about the material presented in this lesson.

Text: Gong and Dragga, *A Writer's Repertoire*, Part VI, "Readings,"
    "Toward Something American," pp. 543–547,
    "Producing a Video on a Technical Subject: A Guide," pp. 557–575.

The readings are written by more experienced writers than the students who wrote the essays in Chapter 12. You will notice, though, that these writers use the same techniques you are learning in this lesson. Your instructor may ask you to read one or more of the essays, or you may wish to read one or more of the essays on your own. If so, the questions at the end of the selections will help you analyze the essays.

Lesson 12

Collaborating on an Explanatory Paper

LESSON ASSIGNMENT

Review the following assignment in order to schedule your time appropriately. Pay careful attention; the titles and numbers of the textbook chapter, the study guide lesson, and the video program may be different from one another.

Text:
> Gong and Dragga, *A Writer's Repertoire*,
> Review Chapter 12, "Repertoire Focus: Explaining a Subject,"
> > pp. 347–368.

Handbook:
> Hairston and Ruszkiewicz, *The Scott, Foresman Handbook for Writers*,
> Refer to the section dealing with the following topic:
> > Chapter 1—kinds of writing
> Refer to all sections in the following chapters:
> > Chapters 5, 32, and 33

Video:
> There is no new video program for this lesson.
> Review of the following video may be helpful:
> > "Writing an Explanatory Paper,"
> > from the series, *A Writer's Exchange*.

OVERVIEW

When you have written a draft of an explanatory paper on the assigned topic, you will be ready for some help from your classmates to improve your paper. There is no new video program for this lesson, and the reading assignment is to review Chapter 12. In this lesson, you will focus your energy on responding to your classmates' papers and on incorporating their suggestions into the revision of your own paper.

Use the "Suggestions for Collaboration" as a guide for your response to your classmate's paper. You may wish to comment on other aspects of the paper, but these questions will get you started. Use the "Suggestions for Writing" as a guide to integrating your peers' comments into your own revisions. When you have finished this lesson, you should be able to respond constructively to your classmates' drafts and to incorporate their suggestions as well as those from your instructor into your own paper.

LEARNING OBJECTIVES

Goal

You should be able to respond to other students' explanatory essays and incorporate peer responses into your own essay.

Objectives

Upon completing this lesson, you should be able to:

1. Respond analytically and constructively to classmates' essay.

2. Incorporate classmates' and instructor's responses into the revision of your own essay.

SUGGESTIONS FOR COLLABORATION

1. Reread the assignment. Does your classmate's paper fulfill the requirements of the assigned topic? Is the topic a "key idea or issue" that is significant to the writer? Is the focus of the paper on the subject rather than on the writer or the audience?

2. Does the writer take into consideration the reader's knowledge of the subject? Do you understand the subject better after reading the paper?

3. How does the writer attain credibility? To what extent is he or she successful?

4. How does the writer motivate you to want to know more about the subject?

5. Mark any passages that could be taken out of the paper. Write a brief note explaining why you think the passage is unnecessary.

6. Mark any part of the paper that could be expanded. Let the writer know why you need more information.

SUGGESTIONS FOR WRITING

1. Make a list of suggestions from your classmates and instructor for revising your paper.

2. If a suggestion appears more than once or if it seems especially insightful, make a note to incorporate it into your next draft.

3. Note sections of your paper that seem to give readers most difficulty. How can you clarify your ideas in these sections?

4. Although you should consider seriously all comments on your paper, remember that you must decide which to act on and which not to.

Lesson 13

Polishing Ideas: The Canon of Style

LESSON ASSIGNMENT

Review the following assignment in order to schedule your time appropriately. Pay careful attention; the titles and numbers of the textbook chapter, the study guide lesson, and the video program may be different from one another.

Text:
> Gong and Dragga, *A Writer's Repertoire*,
> Read Chapter 6, "Style," pp. 163–195.

Handbook:
> Hairston and Ruszkiewicz, *The Scott, Foresman Handbook for Writers*,
> Refer to all sections in the following chapters:
> > Chapters 7 through 15

Video:
> View "Polishing Ideas: The Canon of Style"
> from the series, *A Writer's Exchange*.

OVERVIEW

Style is a quality of writing that seems to be elusive and difficult to define. Yet we know as readers that the style of a piece of writing is often the quality that makes us want to read it—or not. In "Polishing Ideas: The Canon of Style," you will get past the mysteries of style to learn specific strategies that will help you make appropriate stylistic choices for all the writing you do. The lesson does not prescribe "right" and "wrong" stylistic choices, but gives you the information you need to understand the consequences of the choices you make. You will develop a range of styles to suit a variety of writing tasks. You will learn what internal and external forces influence your style. When you have finished the lesson, you will be able to analyze your own writing style and to begin improving it.

LEARNING OBJECTIVES

Goal

You should be able to develop your own range of styles to suit a variety of writing tasks, describe internal and external influences on style, and analyze and improve your writing style.

Objectives

Upon completing this lesson, you should be able to:

1. Define the term *style*, incorporating the idea of appropriateness of style.

2. List and explain several internal and external influences on style.

3. Explain how reading and writing can help the writer develop style.

4. Locate and use usage guides and style manuals.

5. Improve your style by reviewing common style guidelines.

6. Analyze elements of style in professional and/or student writings.

7. Analyze your style in a text.

8. Improve the style of your text by using guidelines from the text.

9. Improve the style of your text by incorporating suggestions from peers and instructor.

TEXT ASSIGNMENT

Text: Gong and Dragga, *A Writer's Repertoire*, Chapter 6

The chapter on style gives a great deal of information of this canon of rhetoric, and suggests many strategies for developing a range of styles. You will need to read this chapter more than once to absorb all the information. Read it once to grasp the essential ideas on what style is, then refer to it again as you work on your own papers and review those of your classmates. For a while, you may need to refer to the style guidelines in this chapter each time you polish a paper. With practice, though, you will learn your own problem areas and you will become less dependent on the text. In addition to the text, *The Scott, Foresman Handbook for Writers* has several chapters devoted to specific stylistic issues. If you need help with some of these issues, use the handbook as an additional resource. Your professor may suggest exercises from the handbook to strengthen your skills in particular areas. As you read the text assignment, use the following questions as guides:

1. What is meant by the term *style*? Why is appropriateness so important in the discussion of style?

2. What are some internal and external influences on style? Explain each briefly.

3. How can reading and writing help writers develop style?

4. Note the list of usage guides and style manuals in the text. Which seem most helpful to you?

5. What are some common guidelines for appropriate style?

VIDEO ASSIGNMENT

Video: "Polishing Ideas: The Canon of Style"

"Polishing Ideas: The Canon of Style" does not attempt to dictate a particular style to you, but rather to give you information that will be helpful in making your own stylistic choices. The video defines style and shows how to make stylistic choices, illustrates the role of style and usage manuals, and shows a professional writer analyzing his own style. Following is a brief description of what you will see and questions to guide your viewing:

1. A documentary focusing on the impact of various influences on the writing styles of a dentist, an AIDS educator, and a poet:

   • What influences do you notice in these writers' descriptions of their styles?

   • What implications for developing style does the expert suggest in the follow-up interview?

2. A scenario featuring common student questions that are addressed by style guides and usage manuals:

   • What are the uses and limitations of computer programs that check grammar and style, according to the expert on style?

   • What kind of information can be found in a usage guide style manual?

   • Why do different academic disciplines use different styles?

   • What suggestions does the expert offer writers who wish to improve their style?

3. An interview with a journalist who uses several styles to suit various audiences and purposes:

- How does the style change with the kind of piece the journalist is writing?

- What seems to be the journalist's basis for making stylistic choices?

- How does first-hand knowledge of a subject help writers develop an effective style?

Lesson 14

Revising for Style

LESSON ASSIGNMENT

Review the following assignment in order to schedule your time appropriately. Pay careful attention; the titles and numbers of the textbook chapter, the study guide lesson, and the video program may be different from one another.

Text:
    Gong and Dragga, *A Writer's Repertoire*,
    Review Chapter 6, "Style," pp. 163–195,
    Refer to Part X, "A Guide to Classroom English," pp. 683–749.

Handbook:
    Hairston and Ruszkiewicz, *The Scott, Foresman Handbook for Writers*,
    Refer to all sections in the following chapters:
        Chapters 7 through 15

Video:
    There is no new video program for this lesson.
    Review of the following video may be helpful:
        "Polishing Ideas: The Canon of Style"
        from the series, *A Writer's Exchange*.

OVERVIEW

Often, as readers, we respond most readily to the stylistic qualities of a piece; as writers, we want our style to enhance our message, not to get in its way. To achieve this goal, writers must be able to analyze the style as well as the arrangement of their own work. In addition, writers must learn to use a variety of styles suitable to varying purposes and audiences. Just as you would not wear jeans and a T-shirt to a formal wedding, neither would you use your informal, intimate style in writing a business report. In "Revising for Style," you will begin the process of self-analysis by becoming familiar with the resources available in your text and handbook. No one can remember all the information necessary to make good stylistic choices; all writers must use reference works such as *The Scott, Foresman Handbook for Writers*. The practice you will get in using this reference will be invaluable whenever you find yourself with questions about style. This lesson gives you an opportunity to learn more about your own style and to learn to control your style so that your writing is appropriate to your rhetorical situation. You will also practice what you have learned about style by revising one of your own essays to make the style more effective.

LEARNING OBJECTIVES

Goal

You should be able to use the information on style presented in "Polishing Ideas: The Canon of Style" and try out some of the techniques for improving your style.

Objectives

Upon completing this lesson, you should be able to:

1. Revise an original essay incorporating information on style presented in the lesson on that canon.

2. Write a brief analysis of your own style based on information in the lesson on style.

SUGGESTIONS FOR ANALYZING YOUR OWN STYLE

1. Try not to be judgmental. Remember that stylistic choices are not "right" or "wrong" but simply more or less appropriate. Choices such as the use of a local dialect might be completely appropriate in some writing situations, but inappropriate in others.

2. View yourself as a scientist gathering data for a report as you examine your own style. Gather your data before you come to any conclusions.

3. Use the "Style Guide" (Fig. 6.3 on p. 191) in *A Writer's Repertoire* to organize your search for data. Use the analysis of Sam's style as a model for your own analysis.

4. For questions in the "Style Guide" that require specific examples from your paper (#3, 5, 7), use a highlighter (either a marker or a highlight on the computer) to identify the specific words and phrases that will help you answer the question. For instance, in answering #3, you might highlight any words or phrases that are local dialect before framing your answer.

5. If you are not sure about some of your analysis (whether a word is part of a local dialect or is universally understood, for instance), use *The Scott, Foresman Handbook for Writers* as a resource. Note that the handbook alerts you to stylistic choices that are controversial or that are especially tricky.

SUGGESTIONS FOR IMPROVING YOUR STYLE

1. Reread the assignment for the essay you are analyzing. List the stylistic qualities the assignment calls for or implies. For instance, if your audience is a college audience, the implication is that the universal dialect will be more appropriate because that is what is expected in a college setting and because college students and faculty are a diverse group.

2. Compare your analysis of your own style in the essay with the list of appropriate style choices you have made. If there are discrepancies, think them over carefully. Have you deviated from the expected style to gain a specific effect or have you simply lost sight of the overall picture?

3. Make any changes necessary to make your style consistent with what is appropriate for your essay. If you have problems deciding which constructions must be changed, consult *The Scott, Foresman Handbook for Writers*. If you would like other views on stylistic matters, consult one or more of the style guides listed in Chapter 6 in *A Writer's Repertoire*.

Lesson 15

Writing under Pressure

LESSON ASSIGNMENT

Review the following assignment in order to schedule your time appropriately. Pay careful attention; the titles and numbers of the textbook chapter, the study guide lesson, and the video program may be different from one another.

Text:
> Gong and Dragga, *A Writer's Repertoire*,
> Read Part VIII, "A Guide for Writing Essay Examinations,"
>   pp. 641–646.

Handbook:
> Hairston and Ruszkiewicz, *The Scott, Foresman Handbook for Writers*,
> Refer to the section dealing with the following topic:
>   Chapter 34—essay examination

Video:
> View "Writing under Pressure"
> from the series, *A Writer's Exchange*.

OVERVIEW

You will face many situations in college and even in the work world in which you will be asked to write on a given topic within a limited amount of time. This kind of writing task is inherently stressful because of the extra restraints of limited time and specified topic, but also because such assignments are often part of some sort of evaluation: a course exam, an important entrance test such as the Law School Admissions Test, or even an urgent but vital assignment at work. The best way to cope with the stress involved in timed writing assignments is to prepare for them and to practice the skills necessary to complete them successfully. That is what you will be doing in this lesson. When you have worked through the lesson, you will still feel tense about these timed writings but you will be able to write an acceptable paper on a given topic within a limited time.

In "Writing under Pressure," you will learn how to handle some of the most stressful—and perhaps most important—writing tasks you will ever face, writing under a time restriction. You are familiar with this type of writing already if you have ever taken an essay test. You may be aware that your state or your college or university has a writing requirement that you must pass to continue your education. You may also know that if you are planning to enter a graduate or professional program, such as law or medicine, the entrance tests for these fields include a timed essay. But did you ever think that after you finish your formal education, you may often be called on to write under strict time restrictions in a stressful environment? This lesson will show you how to cope with timed writing situations and how you can apply these skills from college in other settings after graduation. Besides understanding the place of timed writing within the larger framework of writing tasks, you will be able to analyze topics like those often given on such tests and to manage your time and your own writing process during the tests. These writing tasks will probably still be stressful for you, but when you finish this lesson, you will have some specific strategies to deal with that stress.

LEARNING OBJECTIVES

Goal

You should be able to write "on the spot," whether in the work world or in the academic world, and adjust to the constraints involved in these often stressful writing tasks.

Objectives

Upon completing this lesson, you should be able to:

1. Cite examples of the use of writing under time pressure in work and academic environments.

2. Explain the necessity of writing under time pressure in certain situations.

3. Analyze the rhetorical situation involved in writing under time pressure and compare it with other rhetorical situations.

4. Explain the adaptations of writing processes involved in the essay test.

5. List strategies for writing an essay in a limited amount of time.

6. List strategies for writing an essay test.

7. Write an essay on a given topic in a controlled environment.

TEXT ASSIGNMENT

Text: Gong and Dragga, *A Writer's Repertoire*, Part VIII

The section on taking essay tests will help you in all your college courses that require essay tests. The chapter shows you how to study for a test and how to write an essay on a test so that your knowledge is shown to its best advantage. The chapter explains how to interpret questions properly so that your answers are on target. As you read the chapter, use the following to guide your reading:

1. How must the writing process be adapted to a testing situation?

2. List strategies for writing an essay test.

VIDEO ASSIGNMENT

Video: "Writing under Pressure"

The video for "Writing under Pressure" includes both motivational scenarios and specific information on taking writing tests not available in the text or handbook. You may need to view the program or segments of it more than once, perhaps taking notes the second time. The program includes instruction by professors who are very experienced in preparing students for writing tests, as well as a segment featuring people who must write under pressure as part of their jobs. Following is a brief description of what you will see and questions to guide your viewing:

1. A mini-documentary featuring a public relations director and a computer professional who write under time pressure frequently:

   - How do the public relations director and computer professional handle the time pressure on the job?

   - Does the expert see the situations portrayed in the documentary as typical in the business world?

   - How does audience come into play in writing under time pressure?

2. A presentation by an expert on barrier tests:

   - What suggestions does the test expert offer for analyzing a topic like "One game that is intellectually or physically challenging"?

   - The second topic asks students to agree or to disagree with the following statement: "Other times have had their heroes: Robin Hood, Marco Polo, Joan of Arc, Frederick Douglass, Mahatma Gandhi. Our time, unfortunately, has no heroes. It has lots of charming, glittering people, but nobody to inspire us." How does the writing test expert suggest analyzing this topic?

- The final topic specifies an audience, in this case a parents' magazine, and calls for a multi-paragraph essay: "Many people feel that spanking a child is wrong, because it may have a negative effect on the child's personality. Your assignment is to write a multi-paragraph essay for a parents' magazine in which you explain your position on spanking." What pitfalls are present in this topic? How does the writing test expert suggest avoiding them?

- How does the expert describe what happens to students' papers after they are turned in? How are they evaluated?

3. An interview with an experienced professor who gives suggestions for preparing for barrier tests:

- What common problems with barrier tests does the professor list?

- What suggestions does the professor have for preparing for barrier tests?

- How does the professor suggest students manage their time during the test?

- According to the expert, how can the strategies mentioned for taking barrier tests apply in other writing situations?

SUGGESTIONS FOR TIMED WRITING ASSIGNMENTS

1. Practice, practice, practice. Of course, you will not know the exact topic you must write on until you get to the test, but you can find out what kinds of topics are often used and practice writing on those topics. Use the same amount of time you will be allotted in the real test. Get used to writing under testing conditions.

2. Practice topic analysis. Learn to dissect the writing prompt (the assigned topic) by considering:

   • What aim (expressive, referential, or persuasive) does the topic call for?

   • What audience is specified or assumed?

   • How can the prompt itself be turned into a thesis statement?

   • What principle of organization does the prompt suggest?

3. Practice writing sample essays within the time frame you will be given. Ask your professor or peers to read your paper and to suggest improvements. Then practice again.

4. Read testing guides if they are available. Analyze the sample essays in the testing guide. Compare your own practice essays with the samples. Use the sample topics in the testing guide for practice.

5. Find out the required length of the essay. Then estimate how many pages that will be in your own handwriting. To do so, simply count the words on a page of your own writing. If you write 100 words per page, approximately, you will know that if the essay must be 400-600 words, you will need to write between four and six pages. Then do not count the words as you write your essay.

6. Get together with others who will be taking the same test. Read each other's papers, comparing them to the samples in the testing guide.

PRACTICE TOPICS

The topics below are similar to the kinds of tests you might be required to take. Use these topics as a starting point for your practice sessions. If you are preparing for a state-mandated test (such as TASP or CLAST) or for a college-wide exit test, be sure to get copies of sample topics and essays for the specific test for which you are preparing. If you are preparing for a timed writing as part of your writing course, ask to see samples of successful papers from previous semesters.

Sample Topics for Timed Writings in a Writing Course:

1. Are we ruining our environment? Environmentalists have lots of evidence that we are cutting down vital rain forests, heaping garbage everywhere including Antarctica, polluting our air with chemicals, and overcrowding our cities. However, what does all of this evidence mean to those of us living in our own hometowns? Are we ruining or improving our city or our neighborhoods? Write an editorial for a local paper. Your purpose is to convince the readers of your position.

2. Many people form their opinions of American life from what they see on television and in the movies. Discuss the accuracy of these presentations of American life.

3. We most often think of courage as the ability to face physical danger. But there are other kinds of courage: the courage shown by people who defend unpopular ideas or points of view, or by people who simply meet each day as it comes. Discuss a courageous person with whom you are familiar either through your observation or your reading. Explain why you think this person is courageous, and what effect this person has had on others.

Lesson 16

Reading, Writing, and Thinking Analytically

LESSON ASSIGNMENT

Review the following assignment in order to schedule your time appropriately. Pay careful attention; the titles and numbers of the textbook chapter, the study guide lesson, and the video program may be different from one another.

Text:
> Gong and Dragga, *A Writer's Repertoire*,
> Review Chapter 11, "Referential Aim Writing: An Overview,"
> > pp. 336–346,
> Read Chapter 13, "Repertoire Focus: Analyzing a Subject,"
> > pp. 369–390.

Handbook:
> Hairston and Ruszkiewicz, *The Scott, Foresman Handbook for Writers,*
> Refer to all sections in the following chapters:
> > Chapter 5, 32, and 33
> Refer to the section dealing with the following topic:
> > Chapter 34—literary analysis

Video:
> View "Reading, Writing, and Thinking Analytically"
> from the series, *A Writer's Exchange*.

OVERVIEW

"Reading, Writing, and Thinking Analytically" introduces one of the major uses of referential aim writing, analyzing a topic. The lesson emphasizes the thinking skills that underlie analysis as well as the writing skills needed to write analytical papers. In this lesson, you will see how to think about subjects in a more critical, analytical way than you might ordinarily do. You will see how these skills operate in real-life scenarios, how they can help you in your college courses, and how you can begin to acquire them for yourself.

LEARNING OBJECTIVES

Goal

You should be able to use various perspectives to analyze a topic, with attention both to process and to product.

Objectives

Upon completing this lesson, you should be able to:

1. Define analysis as a means of achieving a referential aim in writing.

2. Analyze a subject from one or more of the following perspectives; importance, composition, development, operation, advantages, disadvantages, causes, effects, similarities and differences.

3. Describe methods for establishing credibility in an analytical paper.

4. Explain how to develop and clarify a thesis for an analytical paper.

5. List guidelines for locating and evaluating information to support a thesis for an analytical paper.

6. List and explain at least two devices for motivating the audience for an analytical paper.

7. Cite uses of analytical writing in the academic, personal, and work worlds.

8. Explain or diagram the rhetorical situation for an analytical paper.

9. Critically read examples of analytical writing.

10. Respond to written examples (professional and/or student) of referential aim writing with an analytical purpose.

TEXT ASSIGNMENT

Text: Gong and Dragga, *A Writer's Repertoire*, Chapter 11

Chapter 11 provides general information on referential writing. Although you should read the entire chapter, the sections listed in the assignment relate specifically to the analytical purpose. As you review these sections, use the following to guide your reading:

1. How can you establish credibility in an analytical paper?

2. How can you develop and clarify a thesis for an analytical paper?

3. Briefly explain at least two devices for motivating the audience for an analytical paper.

Text: Gong and Dragga, *A Writer's Repertoire*, Chapter 13

In Chapter 11, you learn some strategies for writing an analytical paper. Chapter 13 shows how these strategies work in papers by college students. Read the student essays carefully, along with the entries from the students' journals that tell how they approached their writing tasks. Use the questions at the end of each essay to focus your response to that essay. Then think about what you can learn from all the essays.

VIDEO ASSIGNMENT

Video: "Reading, Writing, and Thinking Analytically"

"Reading, Writing, and Thinking Analytically" introduces you to analytical thinking and writing skills. The video explains what analysis is and how it differs from explanation, gives examples of its use, and helps you get started with an analytical paper. Following is a brief description of what you will see and questions to guide your viewing:

1. A documentary showing how explanation and analysis were both used in reporting a tornado and how a college professor uses analysis in preparing instructional materials:

   - Which stories about the tornado are explanatory? Which are analytical?

   - Can explanation be used as part of an analytical story?

   - Why does the government professor ask students for analytical responses to questions?

   - What other examples of analysis does the expert cite?

   - What does the expert say about mixing analysis with explanation?

2. A mini-documentary featuring two people who use analysis as part of their work:

   - What analytical techniques are used by the psychologist and the veterinarian?

   - How does the expert explain the relationship between analytical thinking and analytical writing?

3. A student working on a literary analysis:

- What suggestions does the professor give the student for writing literary analysis?

- What analytical techniques does the student use?

- According to the expert, how does the student make her paper analytical rather than explanatory?

RELATED ACTIVITIES

These activities are not required unless your instructor assigns them. They are offered as suggestions to help you learn more about the material presented in this lesson.

Text: Gong and Dragga, *A Writer's Repertoire*, Part VI, "Readings,"
   "Television Commercials and Food Orientation Among Teenagers
       in Puerto Rico," pp. 547–556,
   "Teaching Maya Angelou's *I Know Why the Caged Bird Sings*:
       A Thematic Approach," pp. 575–582.

The readings are written by experienced writers in a range of fields. The essays relate specifically to this lesson; these essays are examples of the type of writing discussed in the text and on the video. They are professional examples of writing with the same aim that you will be using for your own paper. Your instructor may ask you to read one or more of the essays, or you may wish to read one or more of the essays on your own. If so, the questions at the end of the selections will help you analyze the essays.

Lesson 17

Writing an Analytical Paper

LESSON ASSIGNMENT

Review the following assignment in order to schedule your time appropriately. Pay careful attention; the titles and numbers of the textbook chapter, the study guide lesson, and the video program may be different from one another.

Text:
> Gong and Dragga, *A Writer's Repertoire*,
> Review Chapter 11, "Referential Aim Writing: An Overview,"
>   pp. 332–333 and pp. 336–346,
> Review Chapter 13, "Repertoire Focus: Analyzing a Subject,"
>   pp. 369–390.

Handbook:
> Hairston and Ruszkiewicz, *The Scott, Foresman Handbook for Writers*,
> Refer to all sections in the following chapters:
>   Chapter 5, 32, and 33
> Refer to the section dealing with the following topic:
>   Chapter 34—literary analysis

Video:
> View "Writing an Analytical Paper"
> from the series, *A Writer's Exchange*.

OVERVIEW

"Writing an Analytical Paper" illustrates several uses of analytical writing in the workplace and in college. In this lesson, you will learn the thinking skills used in analysis. You will also see several examples of how these skills are applied to produce an analytical paper. When you finish this lesson, you should be well on your way to writing an analytical paper.

LEARNING OBJECTIVES

Goal

You should be able to evaluate analytical texts in both academic and work contexts, and to draft your own analytical essays.

Objectives

Upon completing this lesson, you should be able to:

1. Analyze a subject from one or more of the following perspectives: importance, composition, development, operation, advantages, disadvantages, causes, effects, similarities, and differences.

2. Establish credibility in an analytical paper.

3. Develop and clarify a thesis for an analytical paper.

4. Locate and evaluate information to support a thesis for an analytical paper.

5. Use rhetorical techniques to motivate the audience for a piece of analytical writing.

6. Cite applications of analytical writing in the academic and work worlds.

7. Explain or diagram the rhetorical situation for an assigned task of referential aim writing with an analytical purpose.

8. Critically read examples of analytical writing.

9. Respond analytically to student writings using analysis for a referential aim.

10. Write a draft of a paper with a referential aim and an analytical purpose, using knowledge by participation, observation, or a combination.

TEXT ASSIGNMENT

Text: Gong and Dragga, *A Writer's Repertoire*, Chapter 11

Chapter 11 contains a great deal of information about referential aim writing in general and analysis in particular. You will want to read the entire chapter, but the pages listed in the assignment refer specifically to analytical writing.   Use the following questions to guide your reading of these pages:

1. How can you establish credibility in an analytical paper?

2. How can you develop and clarify a thesis for an analytical paper?

3. How can you locate and evaluate information to support a thesis for an analytical paper?

4. How can you motivate the audience for an analytical paper?

Text: Gong and Dragga, *A Writer's Repertoire*, Chapter 13

Chapter 13 consists of student essays with an analytical purpose. Read the essays and the accompanying journal entries carefully, using the questions at the end of the essays to guide your reading. Then think about what you can learn from all the essays.

VIDEO ASSIGNMENT

Video: "Writing an Analytical Paper"

"Writing an Analytical Paper" highlights the thinking processes behind analytical writing. You will see how to think analytically so that you can write analytically. Following is a brief description of what you will see and questions to guide your viewing:

1. An interview with an economist who explains how he analyzes complex data to arrive at his theories:

   - How does the economist use the historical perspective to analyze the relationship between the rate of taxation and wages? Why does he think history is important in analyzing a problem?

   - What does the expert say about the economist's analysis?

2. A scenario in which a film student writes a paper using the perspective of similarities and differences to analyze her topic:

   - How does the student use the perspective of similarities and differences to analyze the two films?

   - How does the expert say this perspective translates into the main point of the paper?

   - According to the expert, how could this thinking strategy help in working on other kinds of papers?

3. A documentary about the owner of a scientific research firm and an art critic who use analysis in their work:

   - Which analytical perspectives does the owner of the scientific research firm use in relation to the Tasmanian devil?

- How does the art critic use the perspectives of importance, development, similarities and differences, and composition to analyze the Mondrian painting?

- According to the expert, how can these perspectives be used in writing?

RELATED ACTIVITIES

These activities are not required unless your instructor assigns them. They are offered as suggestions to help you learn more about the material presented in this lesson.

Text: Gong and Dragga, *A Writer's Repertoire*, Part VI, "Readings,"
"Television Commercials and Food Orientation Among Teenagers in Puerto Rico," pp. 547–556,
"Teaching Maya Angelou's *I Know Why the Caged Bird Sings*: A Thematic Approach," pp. 575–582.

The readings are written by experienced writers in a range of fields. You will notice, though, that these writers use the same techniques you are learning in this lesson. Your instructor may ask you to read one or more of the essays, or you may wish to read one or more of the essays on your own. If so, the questions at the end of the selections will help you analyze the essays.

Lesson 18

Personal Dynamics in a Writing Group

LESSON ASSIGNMENT

Review the following assignment in order to schedule your time appropriately. Pay careful attention; the titles and numbers of the textbook chapter, the study guide lesson, and the video program may be different from one another.

Text:
> Gong and Dragga, *A Writer's Repertoire*,
> Read Chapter 3, "Collaborative Writing," pp. 55–76.

Handbook:
> Hairston and Ruszkiewicz, *The Scott, Foresman Handbook for Writers*,
> Refer to the section dealing with the following topic:
> > Chapter 3—draft collaboration

Video:
> View "Personal Dynamics in a Writing Group"
> from the series, *A Writer's Exchange.*

OVERVIEW

The ability to work as a productive member of a team will help you at work as well as in college. Most companies today encourage employees to work together cooperatively to produce the best quality in everything, including written documents. Many college professors now recognize the benefits of learning collaboratively and encourage or even require students to do some of their work as part of a small group. Students have discovered on their own the benefits of study groups and of group efforts at writing papers. In "Personal Dynamics in a Writing Group," you will learn how to maximize your ability to be a valuable member of any group, but especially how to work with a group to produce a paper that reflects well on all members of the group. You will learn how to handle conflicts within the group constructively, how to allocate the work so that everyone does a fair share, and how to appreciate the diversity within a group. When you finish the lesson, you will know how to help your group write a text collaboratively.

LEARNING OBJECTIVES

Goal

You should be able to understand why collaboration improves individual writing skills, how to work effectively in a collaborative writing group, the dynamics of group interaction, and the contributions of computers to collaborative writing.

Objectives

Upon completing this lesson, you should be able to:

1. Differentiate between *simultaneous* and *sequential* collaboration.

2. Explain why collaborative writing improves individual writing skills.

3. Cite ways in which computers have enhanced collaboration.

4. Explain why trust among group members is essential to effective collaborative writing.

5. Follow guidelines for effective collaboration in writing.

6. Respond to a classmate's text in a constructive and helpful way.

7. Incorporate peer and instructor's responses into revision of your own work.

8. Work effectively as part of a writing group.

9. Write a text collaboratively with members of writing group.

TEXT ASSIGNMENT

Text: Gong and Dragga, *A Writer's Repertoire*, Chapter 3

Chapter 3 gives you a great deal of information about collaboration in writing. The chapter will help you understand why collaboration is an important part of the writing process and how to do it well. You will also learn how to function well in a group. The following questions will guide your reading:

1. What is the difference between simultaneous and sequential collaboration?

2. Why does collaborative writing improve individual writing skills?

3. How have computers enhanced collaboration?

4. Why is trust among group members essential to effective collaborative writing?

5. What are some guidelines for effective collaboration in writing?

VIDEO ASSIGNMENT

Video: "Personal Dynamics in a Writing Group"

The video shows people in both the college and the work world collaborating. You will see how successful groups work together. Following is a brief description of what you will see and questions to guide your viewing:

1. Interviews with two students who have collaborated successfully and with a researcher who studied their interaction:

   - What problems did the students encounter in establishing trust and how were these problems solved?

   - Why do the students believe their collaboration was successful?

   - What did the researcher find when he studied the students' collaborative communication?

   - According to the expert, what can writers learn from these students' experiences?

2. A demonstration and discussion of collaboration on writing a grant proposal by an arts group:

   - How would you describe the interactions within the group?

   - Why does the expert think this group is successful in its collaboration?

3. A documentary about an architectural engineering firm that uses collaborative strategies to produce proposals for their clients:

   - Why do the members of the firm's staff think collaboration is such an important part of producing a winning proposal?

   - How does the group handle conflicts when they arise?

   - How does the group avoid the "rush to judgment"?

   - How does this group go about putting together a single document when many people contribute to it?

   - What value to the firm does the expert see in their collaborative efforts?

   - What does the expert say we can learn from this firm about resolving conflicts?

Lesson 19

Writing with a Persuasive Aim

LESSON ASSIGNMENT

Review the following assignment in order to schedule your time appropriately. Pay careful attention; the titles and numbers of the textbook chapter, the study guide lesson, and the video program may be different from one another.

Text:
    Gong and Dragga, *A Writer's Repertoire*,
    Read Chapter 14, "Persuasive Aim Writing: An Overview,"
        pp. 393–412.

Handbook:
    Hairston and Ruszkiewicz, *The Scott, Foresman Handbook for Writers*,
    Refer to all sections in the following chapters:
        Chapters 6, 32, and 33

Video:
    View "Writing with a Persuasive Aim"
    from the series, *A Writer's Exchange*.

OVERVIEW

Much of what we read every day is persuasive in aim, and some of the most important texts we write are persuasive. In "Writing with a Persuasive Aim," you will learn reading skills that will help you analyze the persuasive documents you see every day, from political analyses to charitable appeals. You will be introduced to the basics of persuasive writing: choosing between adversarial and conciliatory persuasion, establishing credibility with an audience, establishing a link with an audience, and supporting your arguments with sound reasoning. You will also see some of the ethical issues raised by the persuasive aim. When you have finished the lesson, you should have a grasp of the basics mentioned above and, in addition, you should be able to describe the three major persuasive purposes (evaluating a subject, declaring a position on a topic, and proposing a solution to a problem).

LEARNING OBJECTIVES

Goal

You should be able to understand the differences between adversarial and conciliatory persuasion, evaluate a specific rhetorical situation to determine which of the major purposes of persuasion best suits the task, and begin the process of writing with a persuasive aim.

Objectives

Upon completing this lesson, you should be able to:

1. Define the persuasive aim in writing in terms of the communication triangle.

2. Differentiate between adversarial and conciliatory persuasion.

3. List and describe the three major persuasive purposes: to evaluate a subject, to declare a position on a topic, and to propose a solution to a problem.

4. Analyze a persuasive rhetorical situation.

5. Explain how to use the appeal of *ethos*.

6. Explain how to use the appeal of *pathos*.

7. Explain how to use the appeal of *logos*.

8. Explain how to prove a claim using persuasive information ethically.

9. Read critically a text with a persuasive aim.

10. Respond to a text with a persuasive aim.

TEXT ASSIGNMENT

Text: Gong and Dragga, *A Writer's Repertoire*, Chapter 14

Chapter 14 introduces the major facets of the persuasive aim in writing. Because the topic is so complex, there is a great deal of information in the chapter. You will want to read it thoroughly before you begin working on a persuasive paper and to return to it as you work. Use the following questions to guide your reading:

1. Which part of the communication triangle does the persuasive aim emphasize?

2. What is the difference between adversarial and conciliatory persuasion?

3. What are the three main purposes of persuasive writing? Define each.

4. How can a writer establish credibility in a persuasive paper?

5. How can a writer establish a link with the audience in a persuasive paper?

6. How can the appeal of logos be used in a persuasive paper?

7. What ethical issues arouse from the persuasive aim?

VIDEO ASSIGNMENT

Video: "Writing with a Persuasive Aim"

The video for this lesson is an overview of the persuasive aim. You will find general information about the persuasive aim, some motivation for learning to write persuasively, and some sense of the complications involved in doing so. Following is a brief description of what you will see and questions to guide your viewing:

1. A scenario illustrating the pervasiveness of persuasive writing and the importance of addressing the audience appropriately:

   - How do the contents of the mail box demonstrate the pervasiveness of persuasive writing?

   - Why are some pieces of mail more likely to be successful in their persuasive aim than others?

   - What other examples of persuasive writing are cited by the expert?

   - What suggestions does the expert have for reaching an audience for a persuasive paper?

2. A documentary contrasting the uses of adversarial and conciliatory strategies:

   - Why did the broadcaster choose adversarial persuasion in the beginning of the battle for the FCC license?

   - Why did he later choose to be more conciliatory?

   - Why does the expert think the broadcaster's choices are appropriate?

   - What suggestions does the expert make for choosing between adversarial and conciliatory persuasion?

3. An interview with a minister/civic leader well known for persuasive speaking and writing:

- What techniques does the minister/civic leader use for gaining credibility, communicating with an audience, and presenting a convincing argument?

- What does the minister/civic leader do to keep his persuasive speaking and writing ethical?

- Why does the expert consider ethical issues to be primary in persuasive writing?

RELATED ACTIVITIES

These activities are not required unless your instructor assigns them. They are offered as suggestions to help you learn more about the material presented in this lesson.

Text: Gong and Dragga, *A Writer's Repertoire*, Part VI, "Readings,"
   "The Phenomenon of Phantom Students: Diagnosis and
      Treatment," pp. 583–589,
   "Six Pawnee Crania: Historical and Contemporary Issues
      Associated with the Massacre and Decapitation of
      Pawnee Indians in 1869," pp. 589–605,
   "An Image of Africa: Racism in Conrad's *Heart of Darkness*,"
      pp. 605–617,
   "Life of the Global Assembly Line," pp. 617–626.

The readings are written by experienced writers in a range of fields. The essays relate specifically to this lesson; these essays are examples of the type of writing discussed in the text and on the video. They are professional examples of writing with the same aim that you will be using for your own paper. Your instructor may ask you to read one or more of the essays, or you may wish to read one or more of the essays on your own. If so, the questions at the end of the selections will help you analyze the essays.

Lesson 20

Writing an Evaluation

LESSON ASSIGNMENT

Review the following assignment in order to schedule your time appropriately. Pay careful attention; the titles and numbers of the textbook chapter, the study guide lesson, and the video program may be different from one another.

Text:
    Gong and Dragga, *A Writer's Repertoire*,
    Review Chapter 14, "Persuasive Aim Writing: An Overview,"
        pp. 397–401 and pp. 404–410,
    Read Chapter 15, "Repertoire Focus: Evaluating a Subject,"
        pp. 413–435.

Handbook:
    Hairston and Ruszkiewicz, *The Scott, Foresman Handbook for Writers*,
    Refer to all sections in the following chapters:
        Chapters 6, 32, and 33

Video:
    View "Writing an Evaluation"
    from the series, *A Writer's Exchange*.

OVERVIEW

Every time you buy one brand of shampoo instead of another, you are, in a sense, evaluating a product. When you read newspaper reviews of books, restaurants, or performances, you are reading evaluations. But evaluative writing is not as simple as it appears; it involves much more than just expressing an opinion. In "Writing an Evaluation," you will learn how to write an evaluation of a topic that is credible and that persuades your reader that your evaluation is accurate. You will learn how to set up criteria by which your subject will be evaluated, how to connect with the audience for your evaluation, and how to base your evaluation on critical thinking. You will see how these skills can help you in your college work and on the job after college. When you have finished the lesson, you will be ready to write your own evaluation of a subject of interest to you.

LEARNING OBJECTIVES

Goal

You should be able to appreciate evaluation as one of the major uses of persuasive aim writing and recognize specific uses of evaluation in work, personal, and academic writing, with an understanding of both the process and the product.

Objectives

Upon completing this lesson, you should be able to:

1. Define evaluation as a means of achieving a persuasive aim in writing.

2. Cite rhetorical situations calling for evaluative writing.

3. Explain how to integrate a subordinate purpose into an evaluative paper.

4. Explain the necessity for setting criteria to establish credibility (ethos) in an evaluative paper.

5. Apply the standards of evidence (sufficiency, plausibility, and pertinence) to the evaluative purpose.

6. List and explain several types of evidence and techniques that may be used to motivate the audience for an evaluative paper.

7. Explain or diagram the rhetorical situation for an evaluative text.

8. Read examples of evaluation critically.

9. Respond to written examples (student and/or professional) with an evaluative purpose.

10. Write a draft of a paper with an evaluative purpose.

TEXT ASSIGNMENT

Text: Gong and Dragga, *A Writer's Repertoire*, Chapter 14

Chapter 14 gives general information on persuasive writing. Although the whole chapter is helpful, the sections listed in the assignment relate specifically to evaluation. As you review these sections, use the following questions to guide your reading:

1. What is evaluation as a purpose in persuasive writing?

2. What are some rhetorical situations that call for evaluative writing?

3. How can you integrate a subordinate purpose into an evaluative paper?

4. Why is it necessary to set criteria to establish credibility (ethos) in an evaluative paper?

5. How can the standards of evidence (sufficiency, plausibility, and pertinence) be applied to the evaluative purpose?

6. What are some types of evidence and techniques that may be used to motivate the audience for an evaluative paper?

Text: Gong and Dragga, *A Writer's Repertoire*, Chapter 15

In Chapter 14, you learn some strategies for writing an evaluative paper. Chapter 15 consists mostly of examples of how students have applied these strategies to their own topics with varying degrees of success. Read the student essays carefully, along with the entries from their journals that tell how they approached their writing tasks. Use the questions at the end of each essay to focus your response to that essay. Then think about what you can learn from all the essays.

VIDEO ASSIGNMENT

Video: "Writing an Evaluation"

"Writing an Evaluation" defines evaluation as a persuasive purpose, shows how it is used in a variety of settings, and gives suggestions for getting started on an evaluative paper. Following is a brief description of what you will see and questions to guide your viewing:

1. Three brief real-life scenarios that illustrate the scope and breadth of evaluative writing:

   • How does each featured writer (the museum curator, the student, and the eye surgery patient) use evaluation in decision-making and/or writing?

   • According to the expert, why is it necessary to set up criteria to evaluate subjects effectively?

   • What challenges do college students face when writing evaluative papers, according to the expert?

2. A documentary featuring a restaurant reviewer who explains the necessity for using criteria and analyzing the audience in writing evaluations:

   • Why is it important for the restaurant reviewer to set up criteria for judging a restaurant?

- Why is the restaurant reviewer so conscious of the audience for the review?

- What other techniques does the expert say the reviewer could use to gain credibility?

- How does the expert say a writer can decide what standard to use when setting criteria?

3. A documentary about the evaluation of a college textbook:

- Why is evaluation such an important part of the publishing process?

- How do the students and the professor who evaluate the text gain credibility with the audience?

- Does the professor have specific criteria in mind when he writes his evaluation?

- What does the expert say about writing for more than one audience?

- What suggestions does the expert have for writers who must write for an audience more knowledgeable on the subject than they are?

RELATED ACTIVITY

This activity is not required unless your instructor assigns it. It is offered as a suggestion to help you learn more about the material presented in this lesson.

Text: Gong and Dragga, *A Writer's Repertoire*, Part VI, "Readings,"
   "An Image of Africa: Racism in Conrad's *Heart of Darkness*,"
      pp. 605–617.

The reading is written by a professional writer, an essayist and novelist. You may not be familiar with the book he writes about, Conrad's *Heart of Darkness*, but he gives you enough information that you will be able to follow his evaluation anyway. Your instructor may ask you to read the essay, or you may wish to read the essay on your own. If so, the questions at the end of the selection will help you analyze the essay.

Lesson 21

Developing and Supporting a Thesis

LESSON ASSIGNMENT

Review the following assignment in order to schedule your time appropriately. Pay careful attention; the titles and numbers of the textbook chapter, the study guide lesson, and the video program may be different from one another.

Text:
> Gong and Dragga, *A Writer's Repertoire*,
> Review Chapter 14, "Persuasive Aim Writing: An Overview,"
>   pp. 395–398 and pp. 403–412,
> Read Chapter 16, "Repertoire Focus: Declaring a Position,"
>   pp. 437–474.

Handbook:
> Hairston and Ruszkiewicz, *The Scott, Foresman Handbook for Writers,*
> Refer to all sections in the following chapters:
>   Chapters 6, 32, and 33

Video:
> View "Developing and Supporting a Thesis"
> from the series, *A Writer's Exchange*.

OVERVIEW

In "Developing and Supporting a Thesis," you will learn how to write the kind of paper often assigned in college courses, a paper that states and defends a position on a subject. You will learn how to find a thesis to develop, how to support it with credible evidence, and how to convince your readers to accept your position. You will not learn a simplistic, formulaic approach to this kind of task, but you will see how other students solve the problems involved in writing a thesis/support paper. When you finish this lesson, you should be ready to begin writing your own thesis/support paper.

LEARNING OBJECTIVES

Goal

You should be able to use persuasive aim writing to declare a position on an issue and analyze texts with this aim, with an understanding of both the process and the product.

Objectives

Upon completing this lesson, you should be able to:

1. Define thesis/support as a means of achieving a persuasive aim in writing.

2. Cite rhetorical situations calling for declaring a position on an issue.

3. Develop and support an appropriate thesis.

4. Differentiate between adversarial and conciliatory persuasion in a paper declaring a position.

5. Explain how to integrate a subordinate purpose into a thesis/support paper.

6. List at least two methods for establishing credibility (*ethos*) in a thesis/support paper.

7. Apply the standards of evidence (sufficiency, plausibility, and pertinence) to the thesis/support purpose.

8. List and explain several types of evidence and techniques that can by used to motivate the audience for a thesis/support paper.

9. Explain or diagram the rhetorical situation for a thesis/support paper.

10. Critically read texts with the purpose of declaring a position.

11. Respond to written examples (student and/or professional) that declare a position.

TEXT ASSIGNMENT

Text: Gong and Dragga, *A Writer's Repertoire*, Chapter 14

Chapter 14 gives general information on persuasive writing. Although the whole chapter is helpful, the sections listed in the assignment relate specifically to the thesis/support paper. As you review these sections, use the following questions to guide your reading:

1. How can adversarial and conciliatory persuasion be used in a paper declaring a position?

2. How can you integrate a subordinate purpose into a thesis/support paper?

3. What are two methods for establishing credibility in a thesis/support paper?

4. How can the standards of evidence (sufficiency, plausibility, and pertinence) be applied to a thesis/support paper?

5. What are some types of evidence and techniques that may be used to motivate the audience for a thesis/support paper?

Text: Gong and Dragga, *A Writer's Repertoire*, Chapter 16

In Chapter 14, you learn some strategies for writing a thesis/support paper. Chapter 16 consists mostly of examples of how students have applied these strategies to their own topics with varying degrees of success. Read the student essays carefully, along with the entries from their journals that tell how they approached their writing tasks. Use the questions at the end of each essay to focus your response to that essay. Then think about what you can learn from all the essays.

VIDEO ASSIGNMENT

Video: "Developing and Supporting a Thesis"

In this video, you will learn about writing that supports a thesis, which includes analyzing the audience, gaining credibility, and developing and supporting a thesis.   Following is a brief description of what you will see and questions to guide your viewing:

1. A documentary about an extraordinary computer teacher who convinced her institution to set up a Unique Boutique for students:

   - How does the computer teacher choose supporting evidence that would appeal to her audience?

   - According to the program expert, what are some other situations that call for supporting a thesis?

2. An interview with a broadcast/print journalist who reflects on his process for developing and supporting a thesis:

   - Where does the journalist get his ideas for the thesis for his column on the two young men?

   - What strategies does the journalist use to motivate his audience to accept his thesis?

- Why does the journalist choose to place his thesis at the end of his piece?

- What suggestions does the program expert offer about developing and supporting a thesis?

3. An interview with a history professor on the process he used to write an article for a historical journal:

- What evidence does the professor use to support his thesis?

- How does the professor gain credibility with his professional audience?

- Why does the professor choose a conciliatory rather than an adversarial tone for his article?

- What is the program expert's assessment of the professor's effectiveness in supporting his thesis?

- What suggestions does the program expert have for developing and supporting a thesis?

RELATED ACTIVITIES

These activities are not required unless your instructor assigns them. They are offered as suggestions to help you learn more about the material presented in this lesson.

Text: Gong and Dragga, *A Writer's Repertoire*, Part VI, "Readings,"
    "Six Pawnee Crania: Historical and Contemporary Issues
        Associated with the Massacre and Decapitation of
        Pawnee Indians in 1869," pp. 589–605,
    "Life on the Global Assembly Line," pp. 617–626.

The readings are written by skilled writers who state a thesis and defend it, the first in a professional paper and the second in an article for a popular magazine. You will notice, though, that these writers use the same techniques you are learning in this lesson. Your instructor may ask you to read one or more of the essays, or you may wish to read one or more of the essays on your own. If so, the questions at the end of the selections will help you analyze the essays.

Lesson 22

Writing a Thesis/Support Paper

LESSON ASSIGNMENT

Review the following assignment in order to schedule your time appropriately. Pay careful attention; the titles and numbers of the textbook chapter, the study guide lesson, and the video program may be different from one another.

Text:
　　Gong and Dragga, *A Writer's Repertoire*,
　　Review Chapter 14, "Persuasive Aim Writing: An Overview,"
　　　　pp. 401–412,
　　Review Chapter 16, "Repertoire Focus: Declaring a Position,"
　　　　pp. 437–474,
　　Read Part IX, "A Guide for Documenting Knowledge by
　　　　Observation," pp. 647–681.

Handbook:
　　Hairston and Ruszkiewicz, *The Scott, Foresman Handbook for Writers*,
　　Refer to all sections in the following chapters:
　　　　Chapters 6, 32, and 33

Video:
　　View "Writing a Thesis/Support Paper"
　　from the series, *A Writer's Exchange*.

OVERVIEW

In "Writing a Thesis/Support Paper," you will learn how to use research to strengthen your central ideas. You will learn how to find material to support a thesis, how to evaluate research material, and how to integrate it into your paper so that the final product reflects your own thinking. These skills are used often in both college and the workplace, so you will see how they can be applied in varying situations. You will also gain skill in the critical thinking skills necessary to produce a credible thesis/support paper. When you finish this lesson, you should be able to tackle a thesis/support paper requiring knowledge by observation as well as knowledge by participation.

LEARNING OBJECTIVES

Goal

You should be able to declare a position on an issue using persuasive aim writing and analyze texts with this purpose in academic, business, and public contexts.

Objectives

Upon completing this lesson, you should be able to:

1. Cite applications of thesis/support writing in the academic, business, and public worlds.

2. Locate information to support a thesis as required by an assigned writing task.

3. List at least two methods for establishing credibility (ethos) in a thesis/ support paper.

4. Apply the standards of evidence (sufficiency, plausibility, and pertinence) to the thesis/support paper.

5. List and explain several types of evidence and techniques that may be used to motivate the audience for a thesis/support paper.

6. Explain or diagram the rhetorical situation for an assigned task calling for declaring a position on an issue.

7. Read examples of thesis/support analytically and critically.

8. Respond to written examples (student and/or professional) of thesis/support.

9. Draft a thesis/support essay using knowledge by participation, knowledge by observation, or a combination.

TEXT ASSIGNMENT

Text: Gong and Dragga, *A Writer's Repertoire*, Chapter 14

Chapter 14 gives general information on persuasive writing. Although the whole chapter is helpful, the sections listed in the assignment relate specifically to the thesis/support paper. As you review these sections, use the following questions to guide your reading:

1. What suggestions do you find in the text for locating information to support a thesis if you need to go outside your own experience and knowledge?

2. What are two methods for establishing credibility in a thesis/support paper?

3. How can the standards of evidence (sufficiency, plausibility, and pertinence) be applied to a thesis/support paper?

4. What are some types of evidence and techniques that may be used to motivate the audience for a thesis/support paper?

Text: Gong and Dragga, *A Writer's Repertoire*, Chapter 16

In Chapter 14, you learn some strategies for writing a thesis/support paper. Chapter 16 consists mostly of examples of how students have applied these strategies to their own topics with varying degrees of success. Read the student essays carefully, along with the entries from their journals that tell how they approached their writing tasks. Use the questions at the end of each essay to focus your response to that essay. Then think about what you can learn from all the essays.

VIDEO ASSIGNMENT

Video: "Writing a Thesis/Support Paper"

"Writing a Thesis/Support Paper" showcases writers who develop and support a thesis as part of their work. They write on widely varying topics for different audiences and different purposes. What they have in common is that each writer must prove a thesis with supporting evidence that readers will accept. Following is a brief description of what you will see and questions to guide your viewing:

1. A documentary featuring an animal behaviorist and a graduate student in art history who research topics by personal participation as well as by consulting articles and books:

   - What kind of research do the animal behaviorist and graduate student do to support their theses? Why?

   - How do their audiences affect the presentation of their ideas?

   - What comment does the expert make about using sources other than library references?

   - According to the expert, what is the best way to gain credibility in writing based on research?

2. A documentary featuring a journalist/college professor who writes for both a general and a professional audience:

   - How does the journalist/professor adapt to a general audience?

- What are the differences between an academic audience and a general audience, according to the journalist/professor?

- According to the expert, what special techniques are needed to motivate an academic audience?

3. A documentary featuring a professional writer who explains how he tailors his arguments to fit his audience:

- Who is the audience for the writer's work?

- How do the writer's personal knowledge and research contribute to his work?

- How does the author say the audience impacts the type of evidence offered to support his thesis?

- Why does the writer choose conciliatory rather than adversarial persuasion?

- According to the expert, what special techniques are needed to appeal to a general audience?

RELATED ACTIVITIES

These activities are not required unless your instructor assigns them. They are offered as suggestions to help you learn more about the material presented in this lesson.

Text: Gong and Dragga, *A Writer's Repertoire*, Part VI, "Readings,"
    "Six Pawnee Crania: Historical and Contemporary Issues
        Associated with the Massacre and Decapitation of
        Pawnee Indians in 1869," pp. 589–605,
    "Life on the Global Assembly Line," pp. 617–626.

The readings are written by skilled writers who state a thesis and defend it, the first in a professional paper and the second in an article for a popular magazine. You will notice, though, that these writers use the same techniques you are learning in this lesson. Your instructor may ask you to read one or more of the essays, or you may wish to read one or more of the essays on your own. If so, the questions at the end of the selections will help you analyze the essays.

Lesson 23

Proposing a Solution to a Problem

LESSON ASSIGNMENT

Review the following assignment in order to schedule your time appropriately. Pay careful attention; the titles and numbers of the textbook chapter, the study guide lesson, and the video program may be different from one another.

Text:
    Gong and Dragga, *A Writer's Repertoire*,
    Review Chapter 14, "Persuasive Aim Writing: An Overview,"
        pp. 397–398, pp. 404–406, and pp. 408–412,
    Read Chapter 17, "Repertoire Focus: Proposing a Solution,"
        pp. 475–505.

Handbook:
    Hairston and Ruszkiewicz, *The Scott, Foresman Handbook for Writers*,
    Refer to all sections in the following chapters:
        Chapters 6, 32, and 33

Video:
    View "Proposing a Solution to a Problem"
    from the series, *A Writer's Exchange*.

OVERVIEW

College professors often ask students to propose a solution to a problem in a specific academic discipline because they know that such a writing task forces students to think critically and creatively. In "Proposing a Solution to a Problem," you will learn the thinking skills you need to know to tackle such a task successfully. You will learn how to write a paper in which you propose a solution to a problem and also how to analyze such papers written by others. You will get tips on avoiding common pitfalls in writing problem/solution papers. The lesson provides motivation by showing you how these skills can be applied in college, at work, and in your personal life. When you have finished the lesson, you will be ready to tackle a problem/solution paper.

LEARNING OBJECTIVES

Goal

You should be able to use persuasive aim writing to propose a solution to a problem and analyze specific texts using the problem/solution purpose in work, public, and academic settings.

Objectives

Upon completing this lesson, you should be able to:

1. Define problem/solution as a means of achieving a persuasive aim in writing.

2. Use invention and arrangement strategies to develop a topic for a problem/solution paper.

3. Cite examples of problem/solution texts in public, business, and academic settings.

4. List and explain several types of evidence and techniques to motivate an audience for a problem/solution paper.

5. List at least two methods for establishing credibility (ethos) in a problem/solution paper.

6. Explain or diagram the rhetorical situation for a problem/solution paper.

7. Read texts with the problem/solution purpose.

8. Respond to written examples (student and/or professional) with proposing a solution as the purpose.

TEXT ASSIGNMENT

Text: Gong and Dragga, *A Writer's Repertoire*, Chapter 14

Chapter 14 gives general information on persuasive writing. Although the whole chapter is helpful, the sections listed in the assignment relate specifically to the problem/solution paper. As you review these sections, use the following questions to guide your reading:

1. What are two methods for establishing credibility in a problem/solution paper?

2. What types of evidence and techniques could be used to motivate an audience for a problem/solution paper?

Text: Gong and Dragga, *A Writer's Repertoire*, Chapter 17

In Chapter 14, you learn some strategies for writing a position paper. Chapter 17 consists mostly of examples of how students have applied these strategies to their own topics with varying degrees of success. Read the students' essays carefully, along with the entries from their journals that tell how the students approached their writing tasks. Use the questions at the end of each essay to focus your response to that essay. Then think about what you can learn from all the essays.

VIDEO ASSIGNMENT

Video: "Proposing a Solution to a Problem"

"Proposing a Solution to a Problem" introduces you to the problem/solution paper. You will learn how to use your own interests and knowledge to develop a topic for such a paper, how to select evidence to strengthen your argument, and how the problem/solution purpose is used in public life. Following is a brief description of what you will see and questions to guide your viewing:

1. A scenario showing a student coming up with a topic for a problem/solution paper:

   - How does the student find a topic for the problem/solution paper?

   - How does the student narrow the topic to a manageable focus?

   - What suggestions does the expert have for finding and narrowing a topic for a problem/solution paper?

2. Interviews with students in history and business communications who explain their strategies for analyzing their audience and gaining credibility in problem/solution papers:

   - Why do the history and business communications professors assign problem/solution papers?

   - How does the business communications student gain credibility in her letter?

   - How does the history student's sense of audience affect the way she presents her solution to the problem?

   - What comments does the expert make about these students' techniques for appealing to their audiences?

- What does the expert say other writers can learn from the experiences of these students?

3. An interview with a political consultant who shares his strategies for presenting his clients' solutions for public problems:

  - How does the consultant use audience analysis in writing materials for the candidate?

  - How does the consultant try to convince the voters of the candidate's credibility?

  - Why does the expert think the political consultant's techniques for motivating his audience are sound?

  - What insights does the expert offer student writers who are working on problem/solution papers?

RELATED ACTIVITY

This activity is not required unless your instructor assigns it. It is offered as a suggestion to help you learn more about the material presented in this lesson.

Text: Gong and Dragga, *A Writer's Repertoire*, Part VI, "Readings," "The Phenomenon of Phantom Students: Diagnosis and Treatment," pp. 583–589.

The reading is written by an experienced writer. Your instructor may ask you to read the essay, or you may wish to read the essay on your own. If so, the questions at the end of the selection will help you analyze the essay.

Lesson 24

Writing a Problem/Solution Paper

LESSON ASSIGNMENT

Review the following assignment in order to schedule your time appropriately. Pay careful attention; the titles and numbers of the textbook chapter, the study guide lesson, and the video program may be different from one another.

Text:
    Gong and Dragga, *A Writer's Repertoire*,
    Review Chapter 14, "Persuasive Aim Writing: An Overview,"
        pp. 408–412,
    Review Chapter 17, "Repertoire Focus: Proposing a Solution,"
        pp. 475–505,
    Read Part VII, "A Guide to Logic and Reasoning," pp. 627–640.

Handbook:
    Hairston and Ruszkiewicz, *The Scott, Foresman Handbook for Writers*,
    Refer to all sections in the following chapters:
        Chapters 6, 32, and 33

Video:
    View "Writing a Problem/Solution Paper"
    from the series, *A Writer's Exchange*.

OVERVIEW

The focus of "Writing a Problem/Solution Paper," is on the more complex problems associated with writing a proposal of a solution. You will learn how to analyze your readers so that your paper will be appealing to them—so they will accept your solution. You will learn how to imagine readers who are very different from yourself and to write a paper that will appeal to such readers. The lesson also highlights techniques for making a logical argument and for evaluating the evidence that supports the argument. You will learn how to sift through your research material and how to select and use only those items that will make a favorable impression on your readers. By the time you have worked through this lesson, you will be ready to write a problem/solution paper requiring outside research and logical arguments.

LEARNING OBJECTIVES

Goal

You should be able to use logic, evaluate evidence, and appeal to an audience in a problem/solution paper.

Objectives

Upon completing this lesson, you should be able to:

1. List, explain, and evaluate several types of evidence appropriate to a problem/solution paper.

2. List and explain several types of appeals that may be used to motivate the audience for a problem/solution paper.

3. Explain or diagram the rhetorical situation for a problem/solution paper.

4. Read texts with the problem/solution purpose.

5. Respond to written examples (student and/or professional) with proposing a solution to a problem as the purpose.

6. Write a draft of a persuasive paper with the purpose of proposing a solution to a problem.

TEXT ASSIGNMENT

Text: Gong and Dragga, *A Writer's Repertoire*, Chapter 14

Chapter 14 gives general information on persuasive writing. Although the whole chapter is helpful, the sections listed in the assignment relate specifically to the problem/solution paper. As you review these sections, use the following questions to guide your reading:

1. What types of evidence could be used in a problem/solution paper?

2. How can you motivate the audience in a problem/ solution paper?

Text: Gong and Dragga, *A Writer's Repertoire*, Chapter 17

In Chapter 14, you learn some strategies for writing a position paper. Chapter 17 consists mostly of examples of how students have applied these strategies to their own topics with varying degrees of success. Read the students' essays carefully, along with the entries from their journals that tell how the students approached their writing tasks. Use the questions at the end of each essay to focus your response to that essay. Then think about what you can learn from all the essays.

VIDEO ASSIGNMENT

Video: "Writing a Problem/Solution Paper"

"Writing a Problem/Solution Paper" demonstrates how to convince readers that your solution to the problem is the best one, and that they can and should act on it. You will see how experienced writers get results from their problem/solution documents. Following is a brief description of what you will see and questions to guide your viewing:

1. An interview with a successful grant writer who gives tips on analyzing an audience:

   - What does the writer know about the audience when he begins on the proposal?

   - How does the writer persuade the audience to take action on the proposal?

   - What other strategies does the expert suggest for getting readers to act on proposals?

   - According to the expert, how can a writer convince readers that the cost or effort is justified?

2. A documentary about an advertising agency that successfully presented their client's solution to a social problem:

   - How do the ads try to convince the audience that there is a problem?

   - How do the ads try to convince the audience to help solve the problem?

   - Why are the ads appealing to the target market?

   - What factors in the ad campaign does the expert think contributed to its success?

- What suggestions does the expert have for convincing readers to accept their solution to problems?

3. A scenario in which a student must select the best evidence for a problem/solution paper:

   - What evidence does the student accept and why? What does the student reject and why?

   - What suggestions does the expert have for selecting evidence?

   - What types of evidence does the expert suggest using, in addition to those shown in the scenario?

RELATED ACTIVITY

This activity is not required unless your instructor assigns it. It is offered as a suggestion to help you learn more about the material presented in this lesson.

Text: Gong and Dragga, *A Writer's Repertoire*, Part VI, "Readings," "The Phenomenon of the Phantom Student: Diagnosis and Treatment," pp. 583–589.

The reading is written by an experienced writer. Your instructor may ask you to read the essay, or you may wish to read the essay on your own. If so, the questions at the end of the selection will help you analyze the essay.

Lesson 25

Revising a Persuasive Paper

LESSON ASSIGNMENT

Review the following assignment in order to schedule your time appropriately. Pay careful attention; the titles and numbers of the textbook chapter, the study guide lesson, and the video program may be different from one another.

Text:
   Gong and Dragga, *A Writer's Repertoire*,
   Review Chapter 14, "Persuasive Aim Writing: An Overview,"
      pp. 393–412.
   Review the sample student papers:
      Chapter 15, "Repertoire Focus: Evaluating a Subject,"
         pp. 415–435,
      Chapter 16, "Repertoire Focus: Declaring a Position, "
         pp. 439–474,
      Chapter 17, "Repertoire Focus: Proposing a Solution,"
         pp. 477–505.

Handbook:
   Hairston and Ruszkiewicz, *The Scott, Foresman Handbook for Writers*,
   Refer to all sections in the following chapters:
      Chapters 6, 32, and 33

Video:
   There is no new video program for this lesson.
   Review of the following videos may be helpful:
      "Writing with a Persuasive Aim"
      "Writing an Evaluation"
      "Developing and Supporting a Thesis"
      "Writing a Thesis/Support Paper"
      "Proposing a Solution to a Problem"

"Writing a Problem/Solution Paper"
from the series, *A Writer's Exchange*.

OVERVIEW

Revising a persuasive paper presents special problems: audience analysis is crucial to the success of such a paper, logical and emotional appeals must be carefully evaluated, and even stylistic choices must be made with the goal of persuading the reader in mind. In "Revising a Persuasive Paper," you will work through these problems in a systematic way so that your persuasive paper will be more effective. You will apply what you have learned about writing with a persuasive aim from the videos and the text, and you will practice using the resources of the handbook to fine-tune your paper.

LEARNING OBJECTIVES

Goal

You should be able to apply what you have learned in the preceding lessons on writing with a persuasive aim and finish your last writing assignment.

Objectives

Upon completing this lesson, you should be able to:

1. Revise and edit a draft of a persuasive paper, incorporating peer and instructor critiques.

2. Reflect on your progress in writing during the semester.

SUGGESTIONS FOR REVISING A PERSUASIVE PAPER

1. Review your writing task. Note your target audience and your persuasive purpose (evaluation? defending a thesis? proposing a solution?).

2. Review any comments you have received on your draft from your classmates or professor. Try to discern a pattern of comments. Mark any section of your paper that seems to give readers trouble. Referring both to the readers' comments and your own paper, try to define the problems with the passage in question. How can you change the passage to reach your readers better?

3. Highlight any words or phrases that bother your readers. Perhaps your language is adversarial when it could be more conciliatory—or the other way around.

4. Consider whether or not you may have used phrases that are offensive to groups of readers; see the discussion of inclusive language in *The Scott, Foresman Handbook for Writers*. Because reaching your audience is so important in a persuasive paper, you may wish to rephrase some of your sentences so that all your readers will feel included and respected.

5. Make the hard choices. In a persuasive paper, it is unlikely that you can please all readers. Refine your paper so that it reflects your best thinking and most creative attempts to reach your readers, but be willing to accept the fact that you may not get complete agreement with your main point.

Lesson 26

Portfolio: The Canon of Delivery

LESSON ASSIGNMENT

Review the following assignment in order to schedule your time appropriately. Pay careful attention; the titles and numbers of the textbook chapter, the study guide lesson, and the video program may be different from one another.

Text:
> Gong and Dragga, *A Writer's Repertoire*,
> Read Chapter 7, "Memory and Delivery," pp. 197–238,
> Refer to Part VIII, "A Guide for Writing Essay Examinations,"
>   pp. 641–646.

Handbook:
> Hairston and Ruszkiewicz, *The Scott, Foresman Handbook for Writers*,
> Refer to any sections that will help you strengthen your writing
> and the presentation of your writing.

Video:
> There is no new video program for this lesson.
> Review of the following video may be helpful:
>   "Rhetorical Heritage, Modern Applications"
> from the series, *A Writer's Exchange*.

OVERVIEW

At the end of a writing course, many English professors ask their students to prepare a portfolio of their best writings for the semester. The portfolio may be a key element in determining the grade for the semester, or it may be used to help both student and teacher assess the progress the student has made in writing. In some departments, the portfolio is evaluated by a faculty committee and is used to determine placement in the sequence of English courses. Whether or not your grade or English placement depends on your portfolio, the preparation of a portfolio of your writing is a worthwhile project. By reviewing your own work, you will be able to assess your own progress through the semester. Looking at papers produced early in the semester allows you to see how far you have come in a few months of intense practice and instruction in writing. The ability to evaluate your own work, to revise it on the basis of new knowledge about writing, and to present your work effectively, will be useful to you both in later college courses and in the workplace. The act of preparing a portfolio of your writing will help you to grow as a person, as well as to develop as a writer.

LEARNING OBJECTIVES

Goal

In this lesson, you will learn how to prepare a portfolio that presents your writing at its best. When you have finished the lesson, you will have greater self-knowledge and also a portfolio to be proud of.

Objective

Upon completing this lesson, you should be able to:

1. Choose and revise work to include in a portfolio.

2. Define the terms *memory* and *delivery* as classical canons and in their modern applications.

3. Identify the two basic type designs.

4. Define leading and explain its effect on the readability of a text.

5. Explain why type that is left aligned with a ragged right margin is more readable than other combinations.

6. List guidelines for the use of illustrations, including tables and figures.

7. Identify three types of graphs and explain when each is used most effectively.

8. Define an organizational chart and flow chart.

9. List guidelines for using drawings and photographs.

10. Explain why and how to cite sources for illustrations.

11. List and follow guidelines for preparing the manuscript of an essay.

12. Revise and edit papers for inclusion in a portfolio.

13. Submit a satisfactory portfolio.

TEXT ASSIGNMENT

Text: Gong and Dragga, *A Writer's Repertoire*, Chapter 7

Chapter 7, "Memory and Delivery," is full of information on presenting your writing in the best possible light. In classical times, when *delivery* meant the oral delivery of speeches, it was the last step in the rhetorical process. Today, we refer to delivery as the presentation of the written work. It is still the last step, but a very important one if you wish to help your readers concentrate on your message rather than on superficial distractions. This chapter is one that you will refer to often as you write new kinds of documents for other courses or for the workplace. For now, you should read it over carefully so that you know what kind of information is available to return to as you need it. This chapter will not help you determine which of your papers to include in a portfolio, but it will be of enormous help in preparing them for inclusion once the decision is made. Use the following questions to guide your initial reading:

1. What was meant by the terms *memory* and *delivery* in classical times? What is meant by these terms today?

2. What are the two basic type designs?

3. What are the most commonly used type styles?

4. What is leading and what is its effect on the readability of your paper?

5. Why should you choose type that is left aligned with a ragged right margin?

6. What are some guidelines on the use of illustrations (including tables and figures)?

7. What are the three types of graphs? When is each most effectively used?

8. What is an organizational chart? What is a flow chart?

9. What are some guidelines for using drawings and photographs?

10. Why and how do you cite the sources of your illustrations?

11. What guidelines should you follow in presenting an essay?

SUGGESTIONS FOR PREPARING A PORTFOLIO

Choosing your best work and revising and editing it are individual activities, but the following steps will guide you through the process.

1. If you are asked by your professor or by the English Department to submit a portfolio as part of your course requirement, the first step is to read carefully all the requirements of the assignment. You may be asked to submit a specific number of papers, to submit specific types of assignments, or even to arrange your papers in a specific order. Be sure that you understand all the requirements before you begin your work; ask questions if you need to do so. Then be sure to follow the guidelines exactly. The

portfolio requirements have been worked out carefully by your professor or by a faculty committee to ensure that all students are evaluated fairly. Failure to abide by the requirements causes problems both for faculty evaluators and for students.

2. Working within the requirements outlined by your professor, choose the work that meets those requirements and also shows your own writing to its best advantage. Reread all the papers that are eligible for submission as objectively as you can. Try to read the papers from the standpoint of your audience. You may wish to review your classmates' comments and your instructor's comments on the papers before making your selection. Remember that the paper you most enjoyed working on may not be your best and the paper that caused the most problems for you may be more successful than you thought.

3. If you are allowed to make revisions to your papers before submission, take the opportunity to do so. You may find that the lapse of time since you turned in the papers originally has cleared your mind and that you will be better able to revise the papers now. Also, you will become aware of how much you have learned in your writing course as you review your work from early in the course. If you find a promising paper, revise it now using all the skills you have gained since you wrote the original drafts.

4. If your professor allows you to do so, solicit help and advice from classmates on your revisions and be ready to return the favor. Remember that your portfolio is a reflection of your writing, not theirs, and that the ultimate responsibility for its contents lies with you. Use the opinions of others a resource, not as a final judgment.

5. Edit your papers carefully. Your professor or the faculty committee evaluating your portfolio will be reading a large number of papers, usually in a short period of time. You do not want to distract your readers from your ideas by superficial errors in spelling, punctuation, or grammar. Use *The Scott, Foresman Handbook for Writers* if you are uncertain about any of these matters. If your professor allows it, ask a classmate to look over your papers just for the mechanics and be prepared to

return the favor. Sometimes we cannot see our own mistakes, no matter how well we understand the concepts of usage and punctuation. If you are using a computer to make your final copies, be sure to use the spell check on your word processor.

6. Make your final copies as neat and presentable as you can. Consult *A Writer's Repertoire*, Chapter 7, for the guidelines on delivery, especially the section on the essay. You do not want your readers to be distracted by the color of your paper or the size of the type. You want them to concentrate on all the interesting essays you have provided for them.

7. When your portfolio is returned to you, carefully go over any comments made by your professor or by the committee. If you do not understand the comments or the grade you received, ask for a conference.

8. After you have finished your course and the grade is final, keep your portfolio. Your first college writing course is an important step in your intellectual development. In later years, you will want to have a record of it.

Contributors

LESSON 1—"RHETORICAL HERITAGE, MODERN APPLICATIONS"

Dr. Kermit E. Campbell, Assistant Professor of English and Rhetoric, the University of Texas at Austin

Dr. Edward P. J. Corbett, Professor Emeritus, Ohio State University

Dr. Cheryl Glenn, Professor of English, Oregon State University

Dr. Gwendolyn Gong, Associate Professor of English, Texas A&M University

Dr. James Kinneavy, Jane and Roland Blumberg Centennial Professor of English, the University of Texas at Austin

Dr. Drema R. Lipscomb, Assistant Professor of English, the University of Rochester

LESSON 2—"THE PSYCHOLOGY OF WRITING"

Dr. William Jones, Associate Professor of Communication Skills, Rutgers the State University of New Jersey, Newark Campus

LESSON 3—"WRITING WITH AN EXPRESSIVE AIM"

Dr. Robert J. Connors, Associate Professor of English, the University of New Hampshire

LESSON 4—"WRITING NARRATION"

Dr. Lawson Inada, Professor of English, Southern Oregon State College

LESSON 5—"WRITING DESCRIPTION"

Dr. Lawson Inada, Professor of English, Southern Oregon State College

LESSON 6—"STARTING A COLLABORATIVE WRITING GROUP"

Dr. Andrea A. Lunsford, Vice-Chair for Rhetoric and Composition, Ohio State University

LESSON 7—"DISCOVERING IDEAS: THE CANON OF INVENTION"

Dr. William Jones, Associate Professor of Communication Skills, Rutgers the State University of New Jersey, Newark Campus

LESSON 8—"ORGANIZING IDEAS: THE CANON OF ARRANGEMENT"

Dr. Robert J. Connors, Associate Professor of English, the University of New Hampshire

LESSON 9—"WRITING WITH AN INFORMATIVE AIM"

Dr. Kermit E. Campbell, Assistant Professor of English and Rhetoric, the University of Texas at Austin

LESSON 10—"INTRODUCING EXPLANATORY WRITING"

Dr. Victor Villanueva, Jr., Associate Professor of Rhetoric and Composition, Northern Arizona University

LESSON 11—"WRITING AN EXPLANATORY PAPER"

Dr. Victor Villanueva, Jr., Associate Professor of Rhetoric and Composition, Northern Arizona University

LESSON 12—"COLLABORATING ON AN EXPLANATORY PAPER"

There is no video program for this lesson.

LESSON 13—"POLISHING IDEAS: THE CANON OF STYLE"

Dr. Sam Dragga, Associate Professor of English, Texas Tech University
Dr. Stephen D. Chennault, Professor of English, Wayne County Community College

LESSON 14—"REVISING FOR STYLE"

There is no video program for this lesson.

LESSON 15—"WRITING UNDER PRESSURE"

Dr. Charles B. Harris, Professor of English and Director of the Unit for Contemporary Literature, Illinois State University
Dr. James Hill, Dean of the School of Arts and Sciences, Albany State College
Dr. Lynn Q. Troyka, Professor of English, Queensborough Community College, the City University of New York

LESSON 16—"READING, WRITING, AND THINKING ANALYTICALLY"

Dr. Drema R. Lipscomb, Assistant Professor of English, the University of Rochester

LESSON 17—"WRITING AN ANALYTICAL PAPER"

Dr. Drema R. Lipscomb, Assistant Professor of English, the University of Rochester

LESSON 18—"PERSONAL DYNAMICS IN A WRITING GROUP"

Dr. Andrea A. Lunsford, Vice-Chair for Rhetoric and Composition, Ohio State University

LESSON 19—"WRITING WITH A PERSUASIVE AIM"

Dr. Catherine E. Lamb, Associate Professor of English, Albion College

LESSON 20—"WRITING AN EVALUATION"

Dr. Catherine E. Lamb, Associate Professor of English, Albion College

LESSON 21—"DEVELOPING AND SUPPORTING A THESIS"

Dr. Sandra Gibbs, Educational Consultant, Urbana, Illinois

LESSON 22—"WRITING A THESIS/SUPPORT PAPER"

Dr. Sandra Gibbs, Educational Consultant, Urbana, Illinois

LESSON 23—"PROPOSING A SOLUTION TO A PROBLEM"

Dr. Marie A. Nigro, Assistant Professor of English, Lincoln University

LESSON 24—"WRITING A PROBLEM/SOLUTION PAPER"

Dr. Marie A. Nigro, Assistant Professor of English, Lincoln University

LESSON 25—"REVISING A PERSUASIVE PAPER"

There is no video program for this lesson.

LESSON 26—"PORTFOLIO: THE CANON OF DELIVERY"

There is no video program for this lesson.